THE TWIN FLAME REIGNITION

Also by Michelle Gordon:

Fiction
The Girl Who Loved Too Much

Earth Angel Series
The Earth Angel Training Academy
The Earth Angel Awakening
The Other Side
The Twin Flame Reunion
The Twin Flame Retreat
The Twin Flame Resurrection
The Twin Flame Reality
The Twin Flame Rebellion
The Twin Flame Reignition
The Twin Flame Resolution
The Old Soul's Handbook

Visionary Collection
Heaven dot com
The Doorway to PAM
The Elphite
I'm Here

Children's Fiction
The Magical Faerie Door

Poetry
Duelling Poets

Non-fiction
Where's My F**king Unicorn?

THE TWIN FLAME REIGNITION

Michelle Gordon

All rights reserved; no part of this book may be reproduced, stored in a retrieval system, or transmitted, in any form or by any means, without the prior permission in writing from the publisher, nor be otherwise circulated in any form of binding or cover other than that in which it is published and without a similar condition including this condition being imposed on the subsequent purchaser.

First published in Great Britain in 2018 by The Amethyst Angel

Copyright © 2022 by Michelle Gordon
Cover Design by madappledesigns, & The Amethyst Angel

ISBN: 978-1-912257-09-6

The moral right of the author has been asserted.

All characters and events in this publication, other than those clearly in the public domain are fictitious, and any resemblance to real persons, living or dead, is purely coincidental.

First Edition

This book is for two Angels who returned to the Angelic Realm in 2017.

Mim. The funniest, most loving Angel to have blessed my life, and the lives of so many others.
Mim, I hope you are having an amazing time with the Angels and Grandad.

And Nanny Marion. The best baker, and hugger I know. You filled my life with chocolate chip cookies and hugs, and giggles that turned to happy tears. You were so very generous and kind, to all humans and animals.

Nanny, I hope you are happy with Les and Bill again, and you're baking a ton of cookies for everyone there with you.

CHAPTER ONE

"I had a really wonderful time in the Elemental Kingdom with you today, Linen."

Linen smiled at Aria. "It was fun, wasn't it?"

"I'm sorry I nearly ruined it by talking to the Leprechaun," Aria said, making a face. "Things really could have gone terribly wrong if you hadn't stopped me. Velvet would have had a fit."

Linen laughed. "But it would have been worth it to see the look on her face!"

Aria giggled with him. "Yeah, it would have."

There was a pause that seemed to go on for several minutes, but really was merely seconds. Linen rifled through his notes. Aria bit her lip before shaking her head.

"Sorry, I really have no idea what the next line is."

"And cut!"

The hair and makeup artists swooped down on the actors playing Aria and Linen and refreshed their appearances while Aria received direction from the script editor.

Violet leaned back in her chair and smiled. It had been

one thing to meet souls who had attended the Academy in real life, and quite another to see the Academy be brought to life with sets and costumes and actors. Yet it was happening. Eleven years after publishing her book, it was being brought to the big screen. And Violet was loving every moment of it.

"Violet, can you just check the next part of the script? We can't decide if it's necessary or if we can cut it down, or cut it altogether." Violet nodded at the script editor and took the pages from her. She scanned through the dialogue, and made a few notes in the margins. She then handed them back and the editor handed the pages to the actress who was playing Velvet. It had been a little unnerving meeting 'herself'. She couldn't wait to see Laguz's first scenes filmed.

She had been away, filming, for a month now, and every day away from her Flame made her feel torn. She knew that what she was doing was important, after all, the number of Earth Angels this film could reach was far bigger than her book could reach. And she still believed that once the Earth Angels were all fully awakened, the world would finally move into the Golden Age.

But she missed Greg. Missed being wrapped up in his arms in the morning, feeling as though nothing else in the Universe mattered.

She sighed and twisted her rings around her finger. At least they were still together, and still strong, despite what had happened in America, two years previously.

The director yelled cut again, bringing Violet back into the present moment with a jolt. She looked down at her copy of the script and tried to focus.

They began setting up for the next shot, which involved a conversation between Velvet and Gold. Violet watched with interest, as the special effects team made the scene work. She had never been on a film set before starting this project, and was amazed and fascinated by the number of people it took to create a film.

An hour later, when the director was happy with the scene, Violet got up to stretch her legs. She left the set and stepped out of the stage door into the bright May sunlight. It was unseasonably warm for England, the weather had been increasingly unpredictable and changeable over the previous few years, and though Violet knew that it was worrying, it was nice to feel a little warmth.

She pulled her phone out of her pocket, and smiled when she saw several messages waiting from Greg, and from Amy. She opened them and replied, missing her Flame and her best friend even more.

She was only five hours' drive away from the Retreat, but the filming schedule meant that she wasn't able to return home to visit, and Greg had been so busy with holding retreats every weekend throughout the spring that he hadn't had a chance to come and visit her.

Aside from missing Greg, life was good. After realising they could manifest what they desired through focused thought, Violet and her friends had quite successfully manifested all they needed and wanted in their lives. Relationships, better health, better incomes, homes, cars, and careers. After Violet had focused on all the things she wanted for her friends and family, she had turned her attention to her own mission. Which involved Awakening as many Earth Angels as possible.

And that was how she was now on set, filming the adaptation of her own book.

After the film was released, the world just couldn't fail to wake up, it wasn't possible.

"There you are! I've been searching everywhere for you!" Violet looked up to see the actor who was playing Gold coming towards her, script in hand. She put her phone back in her pocket and smiled at him.

Time to get back to work.

* * *

"Have you heard from Violet recently?"

Saphron shook her head and picked up her cat, Angel. "No, I haven't. But I imagine she is really busy with the filming at the moment. I think she said it would be seven months of solid filming, then three months of post-production."

Vivi smiled. "How amazing. I cannot wait to see it on the big screen!"

Saphron smiled. "It's the catalyst we need to Awaken the world. And Violet really deserves all of the amazing things that will come from it."

"Definitely. I still can't get over how accurate she was about our Flames. Can you?"

"Considering she doesn't see herself as a psychic, it is. I'm still in shock that mine turned up. And now I can't imagine life without him."

"Life without who?"

Saphron stood up to kiss Sam, a smile on her face. He stroked Angel, who was in Saphron's arms between them.

"Without you. You are just so amazing," Saphron replied.

Sam smiled and kissed her back. "I think you'll find

you're pretty damned amazing too."

"Well of course," Saphron said with a giggle.

Sam turned to Vivi. "Henry okay? Not seen him recently."

"Oh yeah, he's fine. Touch of the man flu, but he's getting over it now, thank goodness."

"Oh, that sucks. Send him my regards. Tell him we need a catch-up."

"Will do."

Sam headed out the door. Angel struggled to get out of Saphron's arms, so she set her down on the floor then filled up her bowl of dried biscuits.

Vivi sipped her fruit tea. "I'd better go soon, I promised Henry I wouldn't be long, and that I'd pick him up some cough medicine on the way home. Poor lamb."

Saphron nodded. "Of course. I need to get some work done anyway. I've got some interviews to edit and post, and some more material to create for my online classes."

Vivi drank the last of her tea and smiled. "No rest for the Earth Angels!"

"Indeed."

Saphron walked her friend to the door, making sure that Angel didn't escape. She didn't want her out on the main road.

She kissed and hugged Vivi, then waved as she got in her car and drove away. Saphron closed the door and went back to the kitchen, where her own tea was now nearly cold. She frowned. Despite things appearing to be perfect, she had a strange feeling deep in her heart that things weren't what they appeared to be.

She and Vivi had met their Flames and they were both

having the most amazing relationships that either of them had ever experienced. They'd never felt so completely at home and at peace.

But something still felt... off.

She wondered if it had anything to do with being on the alternate timeline that Violet had created when she returned to Earth. Violet had mentioned it briefly while she had visited a couple of years previously. Saphron had meant to ask her for more details, because she frequently experienced very strange bouts of déjà vu.

While the thought was still in her mind, she picked up her phone and wrote a quick message to the Old Soul. Perhaps she would be able to answer in between takes.

* * *

"I read about this amazing place, thought we could go there for drinks? I've told Louise to meet us there."

Astrid nodded at Delia, half listening, but distracted by a display of engagement rings in the jewellery shop window they were passing.

When they came to a stop in front of the place Delia had chosen, however, Astrid snapped out of her fog. She stared at the gold lettering on the indigo blue sign in dismay.

"Oh," she said, but before she could protest, Delia was already inside, greeting Louise. Astrid took a deep breath and stepped through the heavy door. She had no idea what to do. She hated making a scene, but how could she sit and calmly drink tea while her Flame was somewhere in the building? She crossed the worn floorboards, determined not to make eye contact with anyone.

She joined the two women at the painted table in the corner, and hugged Louise. The women hadn't seen each other for four years, since they had attended a retreat together. She sat down, and set her bag on the floor, resisting the urge to look around the lavishly decorated room.

"Can you believe it's been so long?" Louise was asking. "I need to hear everything you two have been up to."

Astrid nodded, and tried to smile, but her heart was hammering in her chest, and she could just sense that her Flame was somewhere nearby.

"Let's get some drinks first, shall we?" Delia suggested. "My treat. What do you ladies want?"

"Peppermint tea," Astrid murmured.

"Coffee for me," Louise said with a smile. "Thanks, Delia." She turned to Astrid and frowned. "Are you okay? You look a little pale."

Astrid sighed. "This is Xander's café. He does readings here, and his girlfriend, sorry, his fiancée, makes the fabrics they sell in the gallery."

Louise's eyebrows shot up. "Oh, shit. Do you want to leave? I can stop Delia, we can go somewhere else."

Astrid wanted to leave desperately, but she shook her head. "No, I decided to stay living in the same town as him, so I have to get used to the possibility of bumping into him." She sighed. "You would think, after all these years, that it would be easier? That I would get past it?"

Louise smiled, but her eyes were sad. "You would think that, but sweetie, it just doesn't work that way. I haven't been with my Flame for over twenty years, and I still dream of him almost every night."

Astrid shook her head. "How can you bear it? How do

you stay away from him? Knowing how perfect it would be to be with him?"

Louise took a deep breath, held it for a moment, then exhaled. "I just remind myself that I have a good life. That I have a husband and a home, and that he has a wife and a child." She shrugged. "I would say it gets easier, but I must admit, I would be lying."

Delia arrived back at the table bearing a tray of cups and various types of cake. She set everything down, then frowned at Louise and Astrid.

"I feel like I've missed something, the energy is really weird. What's going on?"

Astrid reached for her peppermint tea, happy to let Louise explain while she did her best to ignore the hammering of her heart.

CHAPTER TWO

"Can you say Dada? Da-d-a."

Charlie gazed into the eyes of his adorable eighteen month old daughter, Juliet, as she stared at him blankly.

"She's a bit young to be talking yet," Ceri commented, smiling at them both.

"I'm sure I was talking by now," Charlie protested. "Doesn't hurt to encourage her."

"She'll talk when she's ready." Ceri shifted about, trying to get comfortable. Charlie reached out to rest his hand on her growing belly.

"Is he moving again?"

Ceri nodded. "I think he's determined to squash my bladder flat. I swear I need to pee again already, and I only just went!"

Juliet climbed off her father's lap and waddled over to her favourite toys, on the mat in front of the TV. Charlie watched her movements, his heart swelling in pride and love for this beautiful little soul that appeared to be calm and loving and patient, all the traits he feared he lacked.

"She's so perfect," he whispered, mostly to himself. He felt Ceri's hand slip into his, and their fingers entwined.

"Yes, she is."

Charlie looked at Ceri. "I still wake up feeling like this is all just a dream. That I never met you, or that you decided not to stick by me, not wait for me. That I'm still single or in prison."

Ceri smiled. "It's not a dream, my love. It's your reality. It's our reality. There was no way I could abandon you, or move on from you. I know that some people may think me crazy, after what happened, but, all that means is that they have never experienced the depth of love that I have for you."

Tears gathered in Charlie's eyes, and he blinked them away, not bothering to wipe them from his face. "I still have no idea how you forgave me. Or how you trust me now with your precious souls."

Ceri looked over to where Juliet played happily, making little noises every now and then. "Because I know that you didn't mean to hurt me, and that you would never hurt her. Besides, you went to all those anger management courses inside, you worked out your triggers, and how to calm yourself down. I'm confident that you will never lose it like that again."

Charlie swallowed hard, a lump having formed in his throat. "I'm still scared that I might."

Ceri shook her head. "You won't. I have total faith in you."

Charlie squeezed her hand. "Thank you."

"You're welcome." She pulled her hand away then shifted forward on the sofa, to haul herself up. "It's no good. I need to pee again.'"

Charlie chuckled and helped her to her feet. Then he got down on the floor, and for the rest of the sunny Saturday afternoon, he played with bricks with his daughter, feeling like the luckiest man alive.

* * *

The sound of Jerry screaming pulled Julie out of her slight daze and back to the present moment. She turned away from the laptop screen just as Charlotte came running into the room.

"It was Daniel's fault! He was pretending to hit Jerry, but then he actually did! Jerry's bleeding now!"

Julie got up and leapt into action, her well-honed mothering instinct kicking into gear. She found the boys outside, Jerry screaming with his hands over his nose, there was blood everywhere. Julie's eyes widened and her stomach turned a little at the sight of the blood. Aragonite arrived on the scene moments later, having run from where he and Greg were working on a project on the land nearby.

"Oh, shit," he muttered. "I'll go get a towel and some ice."

Julie nodded gratefully and Aragonite ran into the house. She reached Jerry and gently prised his fingers away from his face.

"Let me look, sweetie, it's okay, I just need to see what's happened."

When he took his hands away, Julie winced. It looked like he had broken his nose. She turned to Daniel, her eyebrow raised. "How hard did you hit him?"

Daniel shook his head, looking ashamed. "Not that

hard. And I didn't mean to! We were just messing about. I didn't realise he was so close, that's all."

Julie nodded and sighed. She turned back to Jerry. "Does it hurt a lot?" The blood was slowing up, but it still looked awful.

He nodded, his tears mingling with the blood on his face.

Aragonite arrived back, and he quickly wiped away some of the blood, then applied ice to Jerry's nose, making him squeal at the cold.

"Do you think we need to go to A&E?" Julie asked Aragonite. "I think it's broken."

Aragonite studied Jerry's nose and shrugged. "I don't think they'd need to set it, it doesn't look too crooked. Probably best if we just ice it, and do some healing on it, maybe get some of Greg's tea that helps with inflammation."

Julie nodded. She loved how Aragonite always calmed her down, looked at things rationally and calmly.

"Come on then, sweetie," she said to Jerry, putting her arm around him. She glanced back at Daniel and smiled, to let him know it was okay.

Daniel nodded, tears in his eyes. She saw Charlotte approach her little brother, who was now taller than her, and put her arm around him. They went off toward the cabin that Julie and Aragonite now lived in with the kids, in the grounds of the Twin Flame Retreat.

Julie and Jerry reached the door to the house and Aragonite kissed her on the head. "I better get back to help Greg, you okay now?" he asked, addressing them both. Jerry nodded and Julie smiled.

"Yeah, we're good. I'll be getting dinner on soon. You

guys going to come back in?"

"We won't be much longer, I don't think. Greg just wants to get the insulation finished."

"Okay, see you in a bit." Julie went into the house with Jerry, and settled him on the sofa with the makeshift ice pack, and put on his favourite TV show while she made him a cup of Greg's special tea. She added some honey to make it more palatable, and some cold water so it wouldn't scald his tongue.

She set the tea on the table in front of him, then returned to the office, where she had been sorting out the admin for the next Twin Flame Retreat, the following weekend. She sat down, and her gaze rested on the name that had caused her to go into a mini freak out just ten minutes before.

One of the participants booked onto the retreat was David. The man that Violet had met in America. The one who'd invented the dream recorder.

Should she warn Greg? Violet wasn't even going to be there, as she was still filming, but still, would it be strange for Greg to be around the man that Violet had considered leaving him for?

Julie sighed. She could say nothing, but then Greg would work it out, just from his accent and his name. She should tell him now, and then there would be no last minute surprises.

Another thought occurred to her. What if David was coming because he still wanted to be with Violet? Maybe she should tell David that Violet wouldn't be there, perhaps then he would cancel.

Julie nodded to herself. She opened up the email app and quickly typed out a little note to let him know who the teachers would be for the retreat, and that Violet was away. Perhaps he would cancel and save her having to tell Greg.

"Mum?" A small voice called out. Julie closed down the laptop and returned to where her youngest child was. She sat next to him, pulling his body to hers, knowing that she would soon need to make a meal for everyone, but for now, she was happy to enjoy the moment.

* * *

"Thank you so much for inviting us to dinner," Helen said to Maggie, as she placed the bowl full of roast veggies onto the table.

"Of course," Maggie said. "Steve and I love to have you guys over, and the kids."

"Sorry they're a bit crazy tonight, we went to the funfair earlier and they're a bit hyped up on candyfloss."

Maggie chuckled and finished setting out the cutlery. "It's all good. We've got Steve's famous chocolate brownies for dessert, so good luck in ever getting them to sleep tonight."

Helen groaned. "Oh my goodness, last time we had those brownies, I was so full I nearly burst. I'll make sure to leave some space for them this time."

"Brownies? Did someone say brownies?"

Helen squealed as Chad grabbed her around the waist and kissed the side of her neck. "Yes," she replied, turning her head to return his kiss. "Steve's been busy in the kitchen again."

"Ooh, his brownies are the best." Chad released her and went to the sink to pour himself some water. "Those kids are wearing me out today."

Helen and Maggie laughed. "Aww, poor you, get Steve to wear them out a bit."

Chad chugged down the glass of water. "Oh he is, I left him in the garden with them, playing ball. He's about to collapse too."

"Oh dear, well go get them in, dinner is ready. Perhaps after some food they'll calm down. We got some new movies for them in the den, they can relax after."

Helen smiled. "Brilliant. I'll go get them."

She left the kitchen and went through the lounge, and out of the patio doors to the back garden, where her two children were sitting on top of Steve, who was sprawled on the grass. Her first impulse was to laugh, but she stopped herself in time. "Hey, what are you two doing?! Get off Uncle Steve!"

Ivy and Todd jumped up at the sound of her voice, looking guilty.

"Sorry, Uncle Steve," Ivy said quickly, and Todd muttered the same.

Steve propped himself up on his elbows, an exhausted smile on his face. "It's okay, I make a good cushion to sit on." He hauled himself up slowly. "Is dinner ready?"

Helen nodded and gestured for the children to follow her. She took them to the bathroom and scrubbed their dirty hands and faces.

Once she was happy they were a little more presentable, the three of them joined the others at the table, where Maggie had laid out a veritable feast.

"Maggie, this looks incredible," Steve said, reaching out to touch his Flame's hand. "You've outdone yourself, again."

Maggie beamed back at him. "You know how much I love to cook. And to feed my favourite people. I'm so pleased that you guys live so close now."

"Yeah, next time, you'll have to come over ours. I'll get Chad in the kitchen," Helen said with a smile.

"It would be my pleasure, I love cooking. Only if it's stir-fry though. Because that's pretty much all I know how to make."

Everyone laughed. Chad was famous for his stir-fries. It really was all he knew how to cook.

"Have you seen your folks recently?" Steve asked Chad as he helped himself to the roast potatoes, then passed them round the table.

"About six months ago. They still call me Todd, but I think they're slowly coming around to the fact that I'm not him." He sighed. "It was all such a bizarre situation. Losing me, saying goodbye, then days later, losing Todd, but getting me back."

Steve shook his head. "It really is quite miraculous. It must be very odd for them."

"I know it was odd for me," Helen said, spooning green beans onto her plate, next to her roast veggies and nut roast. She looked up at Chad and smiled. "Some days, I can't quite believe it myself."

"Mum, what are you talking about?" Ivy asked.

The adults all turned to the small child, then looked at each other. Helen frowned. They hadn't actually tried to explain to the kids what had happened in Nepal before they were born, and she wasn't really sure they'd be able to explain it in a way that made any sense. How could you possibly explain to a child that Chad's soul had swapped places with his identical twin, and now lived inside his brother's body? Most days it didn't even make sense to her.

"Oh, um, it's nothing sweetie. Don't worry."

Ivy frowned, and Helen waited for her to ask further questions, but her daughter shrugged and dug into her carrots.

Helen looked at Maggie, her eyes widened and head tilted, wordlessly urging a change in subject.

"Funny weather we've been having recently isn't it?" Steve commented, breaking the weird silence.

Helen smiled. "Yeah, it's been really odd."

As the conversation moved onto the weather and local news, Helen relaxed and tucked into her meal, every now and then glancing around the table at her gorgeous family and her close friends, silently thanking the Angels for being surrounded by such love.

* * *

"I really don't see what the problem is," Greg said as he chopped up garlic into tiny pieces.

"Because I told him four years ago that I didn't want him to leave his wife and that I couldn't break up his marriage so that we could be together."

Greg frowned. "But I thought his wife left him? For another man? Which means he didn't leave his wife for you?"

Lisa sighed. "I know. But, well, it still feels weird."

"Why? He's single, you're single, you're Flames, and you still feel a connection to each other, why not give it a try?"

Lisa was quiet for a while, and Greg stirred the lasagne

sauce. She knew her friend had a point, but there was part of her still resisting the idea.

"What are you afraid of?" Greg asked suddenly.

Lisa raised an eyebrow. "Afraid of? Other than being abandoned? Other than him getting ill and dying and I can't save him? Other than the pain that would come if our relationship just doesn't work out? Oh, nothing."

Greg smiled, and tasted the sauce. The smell drifted over to Lisa, making her stomach grumble. She felt bad for burdening Greg with her worries while he was busy cooking for the Retreat participants who were there that weekend.

"It also feels weird, because I teach Flames how to be okay on their own! How to follow their mission and forget about their Flame. If I get together with mine, doesn't that make my workshops moot?"

Greg shook his head. "Not at all. What about when Violet and I split? She was in America and I was teaching others how to have a harmonious relationship. It seemed completely ridiculous, but it wasn't. Because regardless of our own personal circumstances, if we're helping others, none of it matters."

Lisa drank the last of her tea, which was now cold. "So you think I should say yes? To a date?"

Greg shrugged. "If you want to, yeah. Give it a try. You might spend more time with him and decide you don't actually like him."

Lisa laughed. She couldn't imagine that happening. Just the thought of him sent shivers through her body. She hopped off the bar stool. "What can I do to be helpful?"

"You can sort out the garlic bread if you want. And then lay the tables. I think Julia's session will be ending in the next twenty minutes, and it would be good if everything was laid out ready."

"How do you feel this weekend is going so far?"

Greg layered the lasagne sheets with the white sauce and vegetable sauce and sighed. "I'm not sure. I still feel a bit weird about David being here."

"Dream recorder guy?" Lisa had met him earlier in her workshop. She thought he was really gorgeous and had a lovely accent, but didn't dare say that to Greg.

"Yeah. He seems like a great guy, but I can't get the fact out of my head that he and Violet dated, and now he's here."

"But he didn't come here to see Violet," Lisa pointed out. "She's not even here! He came here to learn how to find his Flame."

"I know, I know. Julie and I have spoken about this. It still just feels… strange."

Lisa took a stack of wooden plates from the shelf. "I bet. But Violet has never been strange with me after what happened between us, so perhaps it's time to give David the same benefit of the doubt?"

Greg didn't say anything as Lisa took the plates out to the front room to lay the tables. She felt bad for bringing up their kiss. It was so long ago. But she did feel that David was a good guy, and didn't have any intentions for Violet anymore.

She heard movement upstairs, and a few moments later footsteps on the stairs. She looked up to see the participants filtering down from their workshop.

"Dinner will be another thirty minutes yet," she said. "So you have time to go back to your pods for a bit, or you can hang out here, and I'll get some wine."

"Oooh, wine sounds good," Ailsa, one of the participants said, taking a seat at the table.

"I'll join you," David said, sitting across from her.

Lisa smiled at the two of them, then frowned. She could have sworn she saw a swirling pink light between them. She shook her head and blinked several times. But it was still there.

"I'll get you some wine," she said, as the other participants headed out of the house to their pods. "Red or white?"

"Red."

Ailsa and David both laughed as they spoke simultaneously.

Lisa nodded and retreated to the kitchen. She plucked a bottle of red off the shelf and got the bottle opener out the drawer. She went over to Greg, who was leaning against the counter, checking his phone.

"I don't think you have anything to worry about," she whispered.

Greg looked up at her and frowned. "Oh?"

"I think David has found his Flame."

CHAPTER THREE

"Daddy, why don't you have two legs, like normal people?"

Lily burst out laughing, and Tadhg raised an eyebrow. "You know why, sweetie. I was in an accident before you were born, and the doctors had to cut off my leg. That's where I met your mum, she was the nurse who looked after me."

Hattie frowned and tilted her head. "But why couldn't they fix it? Why did they have to cut it off?"

"It was too badly hurt, Hattie," Lily said, running her hand through her daughter's red curls. "The doctors tried really hard, but if they hadn't taken it away, Daddy wouldn't have survived."

Hattie's eyes widened. "Daddy would have died?"

Tadhg nodded. "Yes, I lost my leg, but I was very lucky to still be alive." He watched the emotions play across his daughter's face and his heart thumped loudly. It was strange for him to think back to the accident. He had been the grumpiest, nastiest, most rage-filled person on the planet. But then Lily had come along and changed everything.

Lily came over and kissed him on the head. "I've gotta go, I'm going to be late for my shift. You two play nice now, okay?"

"Okay, Mummy," Hattie said, her attention already diverted onto playing with her dolls.

"Okay, Mummy," Tadhg echoed with a smile. Lily grinned back, and Tadhg watched her grab her bag and head for the door, off to another long shift at the hospital. Although she loved her work, and she was damned good at it, Tadhg still couldn't help wish that he could do more than just be the stay at home dad, house husband.

Then again, he wouldn't give back a single moment he'd been able to spend with his gorgeous daughter and he knew that raising a child was such an important job. Lily had begun the changes in him, but the moment Hattie had arrived, all sticky and red and screaming, his heart had changed. And all he felt was overwhelming, unbelievable, unconditional love for this perfect little soul.

"Daddy?"

Tadhg looked up, brought back to the present. "Yes?"

"Marnie had an accident, and we couldn't save her leg. She's just like you now."

Tadhg's eyes widened at the sight of her favourite doll, whose leg was in Hattie's hand.

"Oh dear, are you sure there's nothing that can be done to save it?" he asked.

She shook her head, and promptly marched over to the bin in the kitchen, and dumped the leg into it. "Nope. It's too badly hurt."

Tadhg nodded. "How about we make her some crutches, so she can still get around? Daddy had crutches in the beginning, before he got his pretend leg."

Hattie's eyes lit up. "Okay!"

Tadhg chuckled, and he moved from his chair to the floor, where he spent the rest of the afternoon constructing crutches from chopsticks and pipe cleaners.

* * *

Violet slid under the covers, feeling completely exhausted. The day's shoot had been a long one, starting at 5.30am, and ending at 10pm. They had been filming the scenes where the Merpeople were swimming down the corridors of the Academy. This involved huge tanks of water, green screens and a lot of technical behind the scenes wizardry. Violet had enjoyed every moment of it, but she was now completely wiped out.

Before she slept, she needed to hear Greg's voice. She reached for her phone on the bedside table, and smiled when she saw his messages that had been coming through during the day. She opened his contact details and hit the phone button.

"Hey, you." His voice filtered through the phone, and everything in Violet's body relaxed.

"Hey, I've had such a long crazy day, but I needed to hear your voice before I go to sleep."

"What did you get up to today?" Greg asked.

Violet regaled him with the day's tales of mermaid tails, and she smiled as he chuckled at some of the crazier events.

"I can't wait to see it on the big screen. It's going to be incredible."

Violet nodded, even though he couldn't see her. "I know, I can't wait either. Still a good few months to go yet though. They haven't set the premiere date yet, but aiming for sometime early in the new year."

"It'll come quickly enough."

There was a pause, and despite her tiredness, Violet sensed something was wrong.

"Is everything okay? Did the Retreat go well over the weekend?"

Greg sighed, and her stomach lurched. "What is it?" she asked, fearing the worst.

"David was here. On the retreat."

"David? American David? From Arizona?"

"Yes. He booked last minute, I didn't know whether to tell you or not."

"Oh. Was it okay? Having him there?" Before Greg could answer, Violet continued. "Wait, did he pay? Because I offered him a place as my guest, ages ago."

"Yeah he paid. I did mention the free place but he waved it away. I think he did quite well with his dream recorder invention."

Violet waited for Greg to continue, but he didn't. "So was it okay? Him being there? I hope it wasn't too awkward for you?"

"Actually, we got on really well. During one of the dinners we got talking about our inventions, and he helped me figure out how to improve my heating system, make it more efficient and cheaper to make so that I can make a bigger profit."

Violet smiled. "That's amazing. I'm so pleased you guys hit it off. He really is lovely."

When there was another weird pause. Violet frowned. "I'm sensing there's a 'but' through?"

"He met his Flame. While he was here. Her name is Ailsa. She's from Scotland."

Violet's eyes widened and her heart began to race. "Seriously? David met his Flame?"

"Yeah, you could actually see it. The connection between them was palpable. They left the Retreat together, he was going to follow her back to Scotland, spend some time there before returning to the States, if he decides to return."

"Oh Goddess," Violet breathed. "That's amazing! Wow! Did you add that to the score? Of Flames meeting at the Retreat?"

Greg chuckled. "Of course. But, well, are you okay?"

"Me? Why wouldn't I be okay? I'm ecstatic! This is what I wanted to manifest, remember? For David to find his Flame. This is brilliant news!"

Greg sighed, and Violet sensed a huge weight lifting from him. "You thought I would be upset?" she asked.

"I don't know, I just thought, maybe you still felt something for him."

"Oh I do, he is a wonderful Earth Angel and deserves to be happy. But I'm not still attracted to him."

"Okay."

Violet felt her eyes beginning to close, and her weariness threatened to cover her like a blanket. "I need to sleep," she said, yawning.

"Of course. Get some rest. I'm so pleased the filming is going well. I love you."

"I love you too, Greg. Good night."

"Good night."

Violet had just enough energy to end the call, set her phone down, and turn off the light, before her eyes closed and a deep, dreamless sleep took over.

* * *

"Linen! Quick, this side, quick, you've gotta see this!"

Linen crossed the deck of the small boat to where his Flame stood. She was leaning way too far over the railings, her blonde hair whipping around in the sea breeze. He looked at where she was pointing and smiled.

"Aren't they amazing?"

The two of them watched the pod of dolphins swim alongside their boat, and they laughed as they jumped out of the water, danced and twirled.

"They must know that we've come here to help them," Aria said.

"Oh they know," Shelley agreed, joining them by the rails. "They can sense it."

"Thank you so much for having us on this trip with you. I know you don't normally take volunteers," Linen said to Shelley.

Shelley smiled. "I could hardly refuse you, I've never seen so much enthusiasm before."

Linen glanced at Aria and laughed. "Yes, she most certainly has plenty of that."

"Besides, it's something that Angela and I have been looking into, it would help to fund our trips, if we took small numbers of volunteers with us."

"And then we could help more animals," Angela said, joining them on the deck. "I thought here would be a good place to stop and eat lunch, then we can continue on to the cove."

"Sounds good." Shelley reached up to kiss her Flame, and Linen turned back to the dolphins, who were still intent on entertaining Aria.

"Can we swim with them?" she asked their hosts.

Shelley shrugged. "Sure, it's pretty safe in this area, not seen many sharks about. Just stay close to the boat."

Aria nodded and pulled her t-shirt off before slipping out of her shorts. She looked at Linen. "Coming?"

Linen wasn't a huge fan of water, especially not deep water. He liked to be able to see the bottom. He was all for crazy things on land, but in water? Not so much. But he hated to disappoint his Flame.

"Why not?" he replied, pulling his own t-shirt and shorts off. He slipped off his shoes, and followed his excited Flame as she lowered herself over the side of the boat.

The water was colder than he was expecting, and he gasped a little as he dropped into it. He resurfaced and wiped the water from his eyes. Aria had already swum a couple of metres away, and was treading water, waiting for the dolphins to circle back towards them. Linen took a deep breath and swam toward her.

"They're coming!" she whispered loudly over the sound of the waves hitting them. Linen looked in the same direction and saw them coming towards them. His stomach flipped a little, as their fins looked a little like shark fins to him.

When they got within touching distance, Aria reached out, and one of them came to a stop before them, and nudged her hand.

Aria squealed in delight, and stroked its nose. It made some clicking noises, and Aria clucked her tongue in return. Then it turned and began to swim away, Aria took off alongside the dolphin, kicking her short legs as hard as she could.

"Don't go too far!" he called after her, remembering Shelley's caution to stay near the boat. He swam a little way, but then when he looked back to see how far he was from the boat, his stomach flipped and he turned around and started making his way back before the panic set in. He climbed up the small ladder, and hauled himself onto the deck, dripping onto the sun-bleached wood. He looked out to see where Aria was, but she was nowhere to be seen.

"Aria!" he called, his heart beginning to race.

"I'm sure she'll be fine," Angela said, coming up behind him and handing him a towel. "She's pretty strong, and seems to have an affinity for those dolphins."

Linen took the towel and began drying himself. "Yeah, she's like a force of nature. Couldn't stop her, even if I wanted to."

"She's wonderful. If you could bottle her enthusiasm and joy, you'd make a fortune." Angela held out her camera for him to see. "I got some great shots of you two with the dolphins."

Linen squinted at the screen, and smiled at the shot of Aria with her head thrown back in a giggle, her hand resting on the dolphin's nose.

"Those are great, remind me to give you our email address, so I can get copies?"

"Of course." Angela switched off the camera and tucked it away safely. She reached for the binoculars and lifted them to her eyes. She scanned the horizon, and laughed. She handed the binoculars to Linen. "Here, have a look."

Linen put the towel down and lifted the heavy instrument to his eyes. It took him a couple of seconds, but then he saw it. A dolphin with a small blonde woman, riding along by holding onto its fin, was speeding towards them.

He shook his head. She really was the most amazing person. And he was so very grateful he had trusted his intuition and reconnected with her. Even without fully remembering their past life together on the Other Side, he could feel their connection more deeply and clearly than anything else he had ever experienced.

And he wouldn't change it for the world.

When a dripping, giggling Aria finally hauled herself over the boat, twenty minutes later, Linen was waiting for her, ready with a towel and a glass of water.

She let him wrap her in the towel, and eyes shining, she grinned up at him.

"That was magical!" she said.

"You're magical," Linen replied, leaning down to kiss her.

CHAPTER FOUR

Oscar waited impatiently at the school gate for his son, James. He had a whole fun evening planned for them both, including pizza, watching a football game, and then a movie that he knew James had been wanting to see. He smiled when he heard the faint sound of a bell, and then saw the hordes of kids streaming out of the doors towards freedom.

As he scanned the eager faces for his son, Oscar tried not to think about how difficult it had been, only seeing him every other weekend. Since he and Emily had split two years before, he'd only had a limited amount of access to James, and it tore his heart open to miss out on so much of his life. He was a teenager now and was starting to get interested in girls, and was beginning to think about what he wanted to do with his life.

Finally, when only a few kids were left to emerge, he spotted James. He waved at him, then lowered his arm quickly. No child wanted to be embarrassed by an overly keen parent.

James seemed to be frowning as he approached him,

and Oscar wondered what the problem was. He tried to ignore his apprehension and smiled. "Hey buddy, you have a good day?"

"Hey, Dad. How come you're here? I'm going home with Simon." He waved a hand to where his friend stood by his mum's car, waiting.

"What? But it's our weekend? I've got pizza, there's the game?"

"Mum said she'd call you. Sorry, we've got footie try-outs for the local club tomorrow, and we're going to practice tonight. I can't come over this weekend."

Oscar's heart sank, but he nodded. "Okay, sure, well, next weekend instead?"

"Mum's taking me away for the weekend to see Grandma and Grandpa." He gave Oscar a smile, though it appeared more like a grimace, and then started walking away to where Simon waited.

"See you, Dad."

"See you," Oscar echoed.

He watched them drive away, and then slowly made his way back to his car, his feet feeling like lead. He'd often heard of this moment. The moment when your children no longer need you, no longer want you around. But he never imagined it would happen to him so quickly.

Once behind the wheel, he allowed a few tears to fall, as he grieved for the loss of his son's childhood, and for all the moments he'd missed being a part of.

He wiped his eyes with his sleeve and drove home, not at all looking forward to the long weekend on his own.

He pulled up into the driveway of his tiny two bed townhouse, the only thing he could afford after the divorce, and got the shopping from the boot. Looked like he'd be eating the whole pizza himself.

Oscar let himself into the house and dumped the shopping on the kitchen counter. He collapsed into his favourite chair, and allowed himself to stew in self-pity for a while.

Truth was, he was lonely. He and Emily had been together for twenty years, and he'd never imagined that he would have to deal with being single again. But after his epilepsy period, and several near death scrapes, things had changed. He had set up his own business, and started to feel really good about himself, and Emily had fallen into a pit of despair, which led her to fall into the arms of a co-worker. Oscar sighed. He blamed himself. He should have seen how unhappy she was. He should have done something to reach out to her. But he hadn't. And by the time all the details surfaced it was too late.

Emily now lived with her lover and James. And Oscar lived alone. He didn't even have any pets. He basically just talked to himself, like the male equivalent of Shirley Valentine.

Fed up of his own pity party, Oscar hauled himself to his feet, put the shopping away, threw a load of washing in the machine, then switched the oven on. It was early, but he was already hungry.

He grabbed his laptop from the coffee table and woke it up. Oscar opened up his emails, and started scrolling through the spam. In the midst of offers of hot, steamy encounters and penis enlargements, he spotted a familiar name.

His heart began to pound as he opened the email and

began to read.

It was from his Flame, Louise. She dreamed of him every night. She missed him. Even though they hadn't been together since school, and had only seen each other once, a few years back.

He shook his head in wonder. He dreamed of her all the time too. He had kicked himself repeatedly for leaving her, trying to be the macho super hero, and go off to war.

He hadn't realised that she missed him too.

Before he could talk himself out of it, he replied to her email, and gave her his mobile number, in case she wanted to talk. He got the impression from her words that she was just telling him how she felt, and wasn't looking for anything to happen. But just in case...

He hit send then looked at his phone on the table, as if she would pick up the email immediately and call him straightaway.

He shook his head at his own optimism, and continued checking his emails, replying to a couple of work ones, even though it was a Friday afternoon.

Oscar was engrossed in the football match, with a slice of pizza in his hand, when the phone did finally ring, a couple of hours later.

He saw the unfamiliar number on the screen and his heart leapt into his throat. He set the pizza slice down and answered.

"I'm so glad you called," he said, before she had a chance to say anything. "I miss you too."

"Um, Oscar? This is Simon's mum, Nettie. I'm afraid there's been an accident."

* * *

"I'm still in awe that you've managed to capture so perfectly what the Academy looked like," Violet said, as she studied the latest drawing created by the visionary artist for the movie.

Jack smiled at her, then looked around as if making sure they were alone. "I was there, of course."

Violet turned to Jack, her eyes wide. "You were? You never mentioned that before! We've been working on this for months, I just thought you were incredibly intuitive. Who were you?"

Jack smiled. "Green Suede. Professor of Cause and Effect, and closet artist."

Violet's hand flew to her mouth. "Oh my goodness. Suede? Really? I can't believe it!" She thought for a moment about what she had written about him in the book. "I'm so sorry, I barely really touched upon you in the story."

Jack chuckled. "That's okay. There wasn't much to tell. Though if you need any backstory for the purposes of the movie, I would be happy to fill you in." He coughed. "And I didn't mention it to begin with, because, well, I've had mixed reactions when I have admitted who I really am, and even though I knew who you were, and knew you'd written this account of our lives at the Academy, I was still hesitant to share my origins." He shrugged. "I apologise for not being open about it."

"Don't worry, I know what you mean. Coming out of the spiritual closet is tough." Violet frowned, and tilted her head, staring at Jack's face long enough to make him uncomfortable.

"What is it?"

"When I met you I got the impression you were a Starperson. Not an Old Soul."

"Oh," Jack said. "I am both. I'm an Atlantean, like you. I knew Laguz, but hadn't really met you properly, until the end, when you saved most of Atlantis. Though the Academy staff mainly identified as being Old Souls, we had many other dimensions to us." He smiled. "We all had stories, and not all of them were told."

Violet nodded. "I suppose I mostly only told the stories that I would have known, either through first or second hand knowledge. Anything that I, or I mean, Velvet, didn't experience in the Fifth Dimension, wouldn't have been written down."

"Indeed." Jack turned back to his current sketch of the Underwater Garden. "I'd better finish this, ready for the scenes we'll be shooting next month, the special effects guys need some guidance."

Violet watched him sketching for a few moments, still amazed at the level of detail in which he remembered of the Academy and the surrounding gardens. Knowing that he had been there, and seen it himself, reassured her that they were indeed creating a very real portrayal of the Academy and the stories of the Earth Angels who had come to Earth.

"I'm so pleased to be working with you again, Suede," Violet said.

"The honour is all mine, Velvet. We did promise we would be here for you."

Violet left his studio quickly, feeling a familiar prickle of tears in her eyes as she remembered her staff, one by one, pledging to go to Earth to help her with the Awakening.

They had sacrificed their lives on the Other Side, for her. They had trusted that she would follow her mission and make the world a better place.

But was she? What was she doing? Was she really doing enough? Another memory flashed through her mind of her dear friend on a floral sofa on the beach, her bright pink robes rustling in the sea breeze.

It was time to visit Maggie.

* * *

"Come on, we're going to be late." Sarah waited impatiently by the door, while Gold seemed to be taking forever to get ready. The babysitter was already there, entertaining her two children, and she was keen to get going before either of them got upset that she and Gold were going out for the evening.

Gold finally came downstairs, and put his shoes on. She handed him his jacket and wallet, and then headed out the door with him following close behind.

"I'm sorry, I just feel nervous for some reason."

Sarah opened the car and slid into the driver's seat. She waited until Gold was in the car and strapped in before reaching across and patting him on the knee. "It's fine, we're only meeting Hannah and Tim for dinner. It's not a big thing. It's just nice to have the evening with just you and some friends. It feels like we don't get much chance to really talk."

Gold nodded, looking slightly more relaxed. "I know. It will be good. I suppose I haven't really done much socialising."

Sarah put the car into reverse and backed out of the driveway. She laughed. "And whose fault is that?" she asked, checking there was no oncoming traffic before backing out onto the road. "You never leave the house, never want to go anywhere or see anyone."

Gold sighed. "I know, I'm sorry. I still don't feel very comfortable here. I don't know how you adjusted so quickly. Being human is not much fun."

"Gold, you've been here for two years now. It's time to adjust. This is your home, you live here. You are human. It's time to accept it and stop fighting your reality. Start enjoying yourself." Sarah sighed, she was annoyed that irritation had crept into her voice, but despite her love for him, he was beginning to get on her nerves.

"I'm sorry," Gold repeated softly. "It must be hard for you. I'm being really quite useless, aren't I?"

Despite not wanting to hurt him, Sarah felt that tough love was needed to make him pay attention. "Yes. You are being useless. And according to Pearl, you were like this on the Other Side, when I was here, and you were missing me. You're here now, with me, and you're still being useless. It's time to step up and grow a pair. This is a monumental time for Earth. Do you even realise that? What you could achieve here if you set your mind to it? We can't leave it all up to Violet and the other Earth Angels. Or even to the Elders. We need to actively be following our missions."

Gold didn't respond for a while, but Sarah could sense him sitting more upright, and his energy shifting. "You are right, my love." He sighed. "I wish you had said all of this sooner. I have wasted a lot of time."

Sarah smiled. "When will you finally grasp the concept

that time is irrelevant, that how long you have been a certain way is irrelevant? The only thing that is relevant is whether you are motivated enough to first of all decide to change, and then to make those changes happen."

"Wait a minute, those are my words!"

Sarah chuckled. "And where do you think you got them from in the first place?"

Gold laughed as well. "Okay, okay. I will shift myself out of this stasis, and work out what I can accomplish here."

"Good, now, let's lighten the mood a little. Hannah and Tim are having a bit of a tough time, so it would be good if we can lift their vibration a little."

"What's happening with them?"

"Oh, just relationship issues. Nothing serious." Sarah pulled into their friends' driveway, and parked the car. When the engine was off, she looked over at Gold. It still amazed her every time she really looked at him, that he was actually here. Despite his determination to be a hermit and her annoyance about it, it really was something of a miracle to be with her Flame in a human incarnation.

She unbuckled her seat belt and leaned over to kiss him. "Come on, let's be social."

Gold smiled and then kissed her back. "Let's do it."

They reached the front door, and before they had a chance to knock, it flung open and Tim stood in the doorway, a smile on his face. "Sarah! Gold! So pleased you're here. Come on in, we're in the kitchen, dinner is nearly ready."

Sarah nodded at Gold encouragingly, and then followed him into the house.

* * *

Louise stared at her phone, feeling conflicted. Her heart longed to press the green button, and hear his voice.

Her mind was berating her for being stupid enough to contact him. Why stir up all these feelings now? Despite her assurances to Astrid that it was possible to live a full and happy life without a Flame, since their conversation her dreams of Oscar had intensified to the point where she woke up feeling confused as to why he was not lying beside her.

She still loved her husband, but she just didn't have the same deep connection or the same passion for him as she did for Oscar. She glanced at the clock. Her husband would be home soon. If she didn't call now, it would be too late. Before she could think of another reason why she was crazy and should just stop, she pressed the green button.

It rang for so long that Louise was about to hit 'end call' when she finally heard his voice.

"Hello?"

She frowned. He sounded tired, sad.

"Oscar, it's Louise. Um, you said to call if I wanted to talk?" Her hands started shaking a little, while she waited for his response. She could tell that something was very wrong.

"Louise, hi, yes, I did. Uh, it's not a great time, my son, James, he, well, um..."

Louise's eyes filled with tears, and before Oscar could finish his sentence, they were already falling.

"He died," Oscar whispered, the anguish plain in his tone.

Louise gripped her phone tightly, the tears were flowing freely down her cheeks. "Oh, Oscar, no, oh I am so sorry.

When?"

"Three days ago," Oscar choked out. "He was playing ball, ran out into the road, and…"

Louise's heart broke as she listened to her Flame sob down the phone. "Do you have someone with you?" she asked. "Is your wife okay?"

"She's with family. We, we divorced, a while ago."

Louise's eyes widened. She hadn't realised. "Are you on your own?"

"Yes," Oscar whispered.

"Text me your address. I will be there as soon as I can."

"I can't ask you to do tha-"

"You're not. I'm insisting. Now text me your address. I'm on my way."

"Thank you. I'll see you soon."

"Soon," Louise promised, hanging up the phone. Her hands were still shaking as she ran upstairs. She changed quickly, and put on the necklace Oscar had given her, back in high school. Then she went downstairs, wrote a quick note to her husband, then grabbed her phone, keys and jacket before heading out the door.

There was no way she would allow her Flame go through this alone.

CHAPTER FIVE

Lisa sang softly to herself while she got ready, trying to calm her nerves. It was times like this that she really missed her dog, Missy. Just stroking her fur always calmed her down in any situation. But despite her being gone for nearly two years now, Lisa hadn't adopted another dog. She didn't feel quite ready.

Just as she really didn't feel ready to be going out on a date with Joseph.

She glanced at her phone; he would be there any moment to pick her up, and she felt like a complete mess. She finished brushing her hair, reapplied her lip gloss, then sat on the edge of the bed and began doing some EFT. She rarely used it on herself, tending to use it only with her clients. But if she didn't calm herself down, she was going to have a panic attack.

By the time she heard the soft knock at the door, ten minutes later, she was feeling considerably calmer. She stood up, straightened her skirt, and headed for the door. She opened it and smiled up at Joseph, who was holding out a single red rose.

"Hi," he said shyly.

She smiled and accepted the rose from him, taking a deep sniff of it, appreciating the scent. "Hi." She nodded for him to come in. "I'll just put this in a vase and then we can go?"

Joseph followed her into the lounge. He stood awkwardly in the centre while she went to the kitchen to find a small vase.

Her heart was beating fast. Just being in close proximity to him threw her off balance. She took three deep breaths while she sorted out the vase for the rose. She took it back into the living room and placed it on the coffee table. She smiled at Joseph who was still stood there looking out of place.

"Thank you, it's beautiful. Shall we?"

He nodded, and then went to the door, holding it open for her. She gathered her coat and bag from the sofa.

They walked to his car in silence, and Lisa's senses were screaming. His scent, his energy, it was making her whole body wake up.

Inside the car, he turned to her and studied her face for a moment. "I know this was hard for you, and I want to say thank you for giving it, I mean giving me, a chance. I have no idea how this will go, but I really want to see if it's possible."

Lisa nodded, doing her best to remain composed, despite all of the feelings and emotions swirling around inside her. "It wasn't easy to go back on the promises I made myself to stay away from you. I feel like I'm betraying every person I have taught how to be okay without their Flame."

She smiled. "But then I also teach that you should never say never, and that the Universe often has tricks up its sleeve that we cannot possibly predict or conceive of."

Joseph reached out and touched her cheek, and she closed her eyes, the feelings of bliss and peace taking over her nervousness, and bringing a stillness to her tumultuous thoughts.

"Indeed it does," he said softly.

Lisa opened her eyes when his hand moved away. The feeling of his touch still lingering on her skin. "Thank you for being so patient with me. I was just scared. It all feels so intense."

Joseph smiled. "Let's be scared together."

"That sounds good to me."

Joseph turned on the ignition and drove them the short distance to the restaurant he'd picked out. Lisa was still nervous when they went inside, wondering if she would see anyone she knew, if they would think her a liar for getting together with her Twin Flame after she had been so adamant it would never happen.

Her fears were unfounded, and they were seated in a cosy corner, with no accusing stares in their direction. She sat opposite Joseph and picked up the menu, pretending to read it rather than think of something to say.

"Shall I order us some wine?" he asked.

Lisa nodded, not taking her gaze from the menu. Joseph ordered them a glass each, and when the drink arrived, she took a sip, hoping it might ease her jitters.

"Anything look good?" Joseph asked

She nodded, even though she hadn't really been taking in the words. "Sure, I think I'll have the, um," she scanned the menu again. "The mushroom risotto."

"Good choice," Joseph said.

"What are you having?" Lisa asked, putting the menu down and drinking more wine.

"The chicken tagliatelle," Joseph said. "It's my favourite."

Lisa nodded. Her heart was thumping and her stomach was churning. She wondered if it really was just nerves or if her body was trying to tell her this was a bad idea. "Why are you afraid?" she asked suddenly.

"Afraid?"

"In the car, you said let's be scared together. What are you afraid of?"

Joseph smiled. "Oh, the usual things. That you might get to know me and not like me after all. That the connection we felt might not be real. That the connection might be real but be too intense. That the world might end tomorrow. You know, normal stuff."

Lisa laughed and Joseph chuckled too. She felt the tension in her stomach and chest lessening. Joseph reached out to touch her hand, and she felt an electric tingle go through her body.

"Are you still afraid?"

Though the feelings of fear were lessening, they were still hovering in the background. Lisa nodded. "I think it might just take a little time to get used to this, to get used to being with you. But I would like to try." She smiled. "Because I think the connection is very real."

"I'll toast to that," Joseph said, holding his wine glass up.

Lisa picked up hers and clinked it against his. "To real connections," she said.

"To giving it a try," he replied with a smile.

*   *   *

Somehow, even though she swore she would never set foot in there again, Astrid was back in the psychic café. She sat in the corner, and drank her cup of coffee, both excited and terrified at the thought of being spotted by Xander.

Not that she'd seen him in the whole hour she'd been sitting there.

The pull to see him over the last week or two had been so strong that she couldn't help herself. She had intended to just walk by, maybe glance in the window, but then found herself opening the door, marching up to the counter and ordering a drink.

Now she just felt silly. Xander and Kirsty had staff who ran the café and shop, they might not even be there at all. But that didn't stop her from constantly scanning the room, hopeful for a glimpse of him.

Despite being a sunny Thursday, it was really busy, and Astrid felt proud of Xander for creating a thriving business, especially in the current economic climate.

"That was amazing! Xander was so accurate!"

Nearly spilling her coffee at the sound of his name, Astrid looked up to see a woman enter the café from the back room, and join her friend at a nearby table.

So Xander was there. He was doing readings.

Astrid set her cup down. She knew that she shouldn't. She knew it would be a bad idea, but ever since the Christmas Party where he had so clearly recognised her, but refused to engage with her, she had wanted to know why.

Why didn't he want to be with her? Was it just because of Kirsty, or was there another reason?

With these thoughts whirling around, she got up and went to the counter.

"Are there any appointments free for readings?" she found herself asking the girl behind the counter.

The girl grabbed a black notebook and scanned the page, then looked at the clock.

"Yes, there is, right now. You pay now, then just go through there."

Astrid looked at the door and gulped. Part of her had hoped the answer would be no, and then she could leave quickly, knowing that she had at least tried. "Okay, um, yeah." She dug around in her bag and pulled out her credit card. She handed it over, paid, and then with her heart thumping like a bass drum in her chest, she went through the purple door.

She blinked a little in the gloomy hallway beyond, trying to get her bearings. She walked slowly, and then came to another door at the end.

She took a deep breath and knocked. Her heart stalled when she heard Xander call out to enter. Would he even remember her? Would he know who she was?

Before she could turn around and run, she pushed the door open and stepped inside. She glanced around, taking in the draped fabrics and artwork on the walls. She looked at Xander, who was sat at a table in the centre of the room. Their eyes met, and his hands paused in their shuffling of tarot cards.

"Astrid?"

Astrid smiled and nodded slightly. "Hi, Xander."

There was a long pause. The air between them seemed to crackle with tension and attraction.

"Please, sit down."

Astrid sat down, clutching her bag on her lap. "How are you?" she asked. "Haven't seen you since the party... This place is amazing. I hope it's going well." Aware that she was babbling, Astrid closed her mouth tightly.

"Thank you, it's been hard work, but it's really been going well in the last year. Um, how are you?"

"Good," Astrid managed to say past the lump in her throat.

"Good," Xander echoed. "Um, you wanted a reading?"

Astrid nodded, even though she didn't really. What she actually wanted was to lean over the table and kiss her Twin Flame.

Xander resumed shuffling the cards, then asked her to pick out seven random cards. When he laid them out on the table, one by one, Astrid noticed his eyes growing wide.

"What is it?" she asked, a little afraid to find out.

Xander looked up over her shoulder, and then looked to his right side, appearing to have some kind of internal conversation with himself. After a few moments, his attention focussed back on Astrid.

"Why did you come in here today?"

Astrid frowned. "I don't know. I keep... dreaming of you. The pull was really strong. Even after all this time."

Xander looked back at the cards, then up at Astrid. "It wasn't because you heard about Kirsty?"

Astrid shook her head. "No, what do you mean?"

"Kirsty was offered a job in New York with a big fashion company. She didn't want me to have to wait for her, so we split up."

Astrid's mouth popped open in shock and her heart began hammering again. "Oh," she said. "I'm sorry, I didn't know."

"I know. I can see that. Which is why..." He glanced over her shoulder again, and to his side. "How didn't I see this coming?" he muttered.

"See what?" she asked.

He looked directly into her eyes. "You. When we last met, the cards, the Angels, all the signs said it would be a bad idea. For both of us. But now... Things seem to have changed, and I have no idea why."

"Changed? What are the cards saying now?"

"That it will work. That we would be happy, together."

A tear slid down Astrid's cheek, and she reached across the table to touch Xander's shaking hand.

He wrapped his fingers around hers, and her heart calmed down. "How do you feel about that?" she asked.

"Shocked," he admitted. "But also… excited." He stood up, his hand still holding hers. She stood up too, and he slowly pulled her toward him. He released her hand and pulled her in close, wrapping his arms around her waist and holding her tight to his chest.

And with that one hug, Astrid knew that she had finally come home.

* * *

"So you may all be wondering why I invited you all here for this Spiritual Sisters reunion," Maggie began, looking around the room at Keeley, Fay, Beattie, Leila, and also Helen.

"You mean it wasn't just because you missed us all desperately?" Beattie asked.

The women laughed.

"Well, aside from that, I was contacted by a very dear friend of ours, and I thought it would be a good idea to get everyone together again."

"Hey, everyone."

Keeley jumped up off the sofa and launched herself into Violet's arms. "Oh my goodness! It's been too long!"

Violet laughed and hugged her sister tightly. "I know, I know. I'm so sorry, life got a little crazy."

The other women all got up and engulfed the two of them in a huge group hug.

Maggie watched them, a smile on her face. It really had been too long since they'd all seen each other. She was pleased she had invited them all over Suddenly, the living room disappeared around her, and her gaze shifted.

She could see Greg, Keeley and her Flame, Karl, and herself and Steve, and Leila and Beattie all sitting in the audience of a huge theatre, while Violet stood on stage. Everyone looked a little older, but otherwise the same as they did right now.

"Even if this is the end," Violet said, her voice ringing out clearly. "It will all work out just fine. There is nothing to fear, no darkness to endure, nothing to lose. When we awake tomorrow morning, we will either be on the Other Side, or we will have just entered the Golden Age. Either way, I will see you again."

"Maggie?"

Maggie blinked and the stage and the theatre disappeared, and a younger, worried-looking Violet was peering at her.

"Yes, I'm okay," Maggie replied automatically.

"You're crying," Violet said softly, holding a tissue out to her friend.

Maggie took it and dabbed her eyes. She forced a smile. "It's okay, was just a strange vision."

Violet nodded, but didn't push her for further information. Instead, she turned to the other women and offered to get them more drinks, stepping up as the hostess while Maggie went to the bathroom to collect herself.

It had been a while since she'd had a vision, so it had caught her off guard. But it also upset her. Was that really their future? In maybe a decade or so? The end of the world or a possible Golden Age? Was that the best that they had managed to create? Maggie had been so sure that this alternate timeline would turn out to be so much better than the first. That Violet's decision to remain on Earth would shift everything. But it seemed like she had been wrong.

Maggie looked at her reflection in the mirror, and felt a heaviness in her heart. The sound of laughter filtered into her consciousness, and she splashed some water on her face, then took a few deep breaths before re-joining the others.

"Are you sure you're okay?" Violet asked, a few hours later as they washed up the wine glasses and dishes.

Maggie nodded. "Yes, I'm sorry, I wasn't very present tonight, was I?"

"If you want to talk about the vision, I'm here."

"I know. It wasn't a bad vision, it just unsettled me a little. But actually, what I want to talk about is you. You told us all how the film is going, and it sounds amazing, but I can sense that there's something you feel strange about?"

Violet smiled at her friend. "I had forgotten how perceptive you are. Yes, the other day, after meeting with the conceptual artist – who was a professor at the Academy, by the way – I was suddenly struck with the thought that well, maybe I'm just not doing enough."

Maggie frowned and placed another glass on the rack for Violet to dry. "What do you mean?"

Violet sighed. "It just doesn't feel like writing my book, and making this movie of it, is enough. To shift things. To Awaken the world. To take us into the Golden Age. And maybe it's because I've been so wrapped up in my own dramas. With Greg, and the Retreat, and with financial stuff. I don't know. But it feels like it's all too little, that things are changing, maybe, but at the pace of a snail." Violet shook her head. "I don't know, maybe I'm just being silly. After all, I don't know what else I could be doing to change things."

Maggie washed up three more glasses before she spoke. "I know what you mean. My vision, before, well, it was a bit like that."

"Oh? What happened?"

Maggie frowned, feeling like the details weren't hers to share, but that the feeling of it was important. "That we haven't done enough. That the world may not Awaken. That things might just stay the same."

"So I guess coming back from the dead and going back in time by twenty years wasn't enough huh?" Violet said jokingly as she carefully put the glasses back in the cupboard.

Maggie chuckled. "I guess not. But then, I'm not sure if it matters?"

"What do you mean?"

"Look at what we have achieved – the Flames reuniting, the Earth Angels waking up, it's all pretty amazing. And much of that didn't happen in the original timeline. Perhaps we should just be thankful that in the end, we are all together."

Violet smiled. "You saw us all, there? Together?"

Maggie nodded. "Yes. I did."

Maggie could see the deep relief on Violet's face, and she wondered if her friend still feared losing Greg.

"That's good enough for me," Violet said softly.

Maggie held her arms open and they hugged.

"Me too," she replied. But deep in her heart, she knew it was a lie.

CHAPTER SIX

"What are you working on?"

Sam looked up from his work and smiled at Saphron. "Oh, just tinkering with an idea. You know me." He set down his tools and stood up from his workbench to pull Saphron into his arms. "It might be time for a break though?" He smiled mischievously at her, making her giggle.

"Sounds like a good idea to me." She reached up to kiss him, and melted into his embrace. When Violet had predicted, two years ago, that Saphron would meet her Flame, she'd had no idea how incredible it would be.

Sam pulled back a little and stared into her eyes. "Where did you go?"

Saphron shook her head. They were so connected; he could tell instantly when she was no longer in the present moment.

"I was thinking of Violet, and how she told me I would meet you," she replied.

"I would love to meet Violet one day. I think I remember her."

Saphron frowned. "You do? You haven't mentioned that before."

"I realised just the other day. I was looking at that photo of you and her and Vivi, and I had a flashback of when we were all in Atlantis."

Saphron's eyes widened. "Oh, wow. You knew her then?"

"Kind of. I knew her Flame, Laguz. We were in a healing group together. Along with Henry, whose name was Wunjo, and five other men: Dagaz, Berkana, Inguz, Kaunaz and Jera."

"Runes! How funny, even though I knew your name and Greg's, it hadn't clicked that perhaps there would be more souls with runic names."

Sam smiled. "It hadn't really occurred to me either. But when I had this memory pop up, of this circle of men, I instinctively knew their names. And it wasn't until I searched for the meanings online that I realised they were runes. It's not something I've ever studied before."

"So do you think the others are here? On Earth?"

"Yes, I do, and I get the feeling I will meet them all soon. That there is something important we are meant to achieve together."

Saphron was quiet for a few moments while she considered this. It did seem strange that these memories were rising to the surface now, and that Sam had known Greg in Atlantis, and she had known Violet in the Academy. "Do you have any ideas? What it means?"

Sam shook his head. "No, but I have been thinking, how do you feel about visiting Violet sometime?"

Saphron gasped. "In the UK? Are you serious? I would love to! Visit the Twin Flame Retreat? Meet Julie and Greg and Lisa and so many others from the Academy? That would be incredible!"

Sam nodded. "I'll see what I can do with time off work. But I think we should go quite soon. Maybe when Violet has finished filming and is home again?"

Saphron grinned. "I'll start looking at flights!" She kissed him quickly and pulled away to head back into the house. But Sam pulled her back to him again.

"We have time," he murmured into her ear. "I have other plans for you first."

He leaned down to kiss her, and once again, she lost herself in his embrace.

* * *

"I'm here, I'm right here, baby, just stay with me, okay?"

Ceri's eyes remained locked on his while the doctors and nurses worked feverishly around them to deliver their child safely. What had started off as a routine natural birth had changed to an emergency caesarean section when the baby became bradycardic during contractions.

"I'm scared," Ceri whispered, tears running down the side of her face. "Please let our baby be okay."

"He's going to be just fine," Charlie promised, although he had no idea if that were true, he felt just as terrified as his Flame.

There was a hush in the bustle for a moment, and Charlie looked around the partition to see their little baby boy being lifted up out of Ceri's abdomen.

There was no sound.

Charlie's breathing became shallow as he watched the

team whisk him away and begin to clear his airway and start resuscitation. They worked hard for several minutes, before they stepped back, heads bowed. Charlie shook his head. "No," he whispered. He let go of Ceri's hand and went over to where he was being cleaned up and wrapped in a cloth.

"Why are you giving up? Keep going!"

"I'm sorry, Charlie. He's gone." The doctor truly looked heartbroken. "There's nothing more we can do."

"No, there must be. No! What happened? What happened!" Charlie reached out to touch his baby boy's perfect round cheek. His lips were a dark blue. Charlie dropped to his knees, and began to sob. He couldn't hear any of the words coming from the doctor. The grief had engulfed him.

"Charlie?" Ceri called out.

His heart shattered. Charlie accepted the nurses help to get back to his feet. He returned to Ceri, whose eyes were wide open in terror and disbelief. He shook his head, his eyes full of grief. "He's with the Angels, baby."

Ceri's face crumpled and she let out a wail, the reality setting in. Charlie sat back next to her, and gripped her hand in his. He lay his head on her shoulder and they cried together. They cried for their little boy who hadn't had the chance to draw his first breath.

It felt like both hours and only minutes later when they had finished operating, and were ready to take Ceri back to a private room. By now, her sobs had calmed down to sniffles, and Charlie had managed to hold himself together for the short walk.

Once alone, Charlie sat on the edge of the bed and gripped her hand tightly. "I love you," he said. "I am so, so sorry."

Ceri shook her head.

"What if it was karma? Punishment for all the things I've done wrong?"

She shook her head again, unable to form words.

Charlie bowed his head, and let his tears fall. He felt so guilty, and he couldn't seem to shift it.

"Hey."

They both looked up to see the nurse from the theatre standing there. A blue bundle in her arms. "Would you like to see him?"

Ceri brightened at the prospect. She desperately wanted to hold her son. She nodded and held her hands out, and Charlie sat in the chair next to the bed. The nurse came over to the bed, and held out their baby boy to Ceri. She took him and nestled him in her arms. Aside from his tiny blue lips, he looked as though he could be sleeping. Ceri's tears fell freely onto his forehead, and soaked into the blue blanket.

Charlie reached out to stroke his tiny cheek. Neither of them noticed the nurse respectfully leaving them alone.

"He's so perfect," Ceri said, her tears flowing faster. "Juliet would have loved him."

Charlie's heart broke again at the idea of having to explain, somehow, that Juliet wouldn't be a big sister. Part of him hoped that she just wouldn't understand.

"What should we call him?" Ceri whispered.

Charlie frowned. "Call him?"

"He still needs a name. He may not have lived on this planet, but he lived within me for nine months. He needs a name."

Charlie grabbed a tissue from the side of the bed to blow his nose. "You're right, he does. What are you thinking?"

"I think he looks like a William to me."

Charlie smiled and nodded. "William. That's perfect."

Ceri smiled at him, then rocked her little boy in her arms. "Sleep, my little William. Sleep. And say hello to the Angels for me."

* * *

"And action!"

The moment the music began, the hairs on Violet's arms stood up. She hadn't heard the Moonlight Sonata since Greg had played it twelve years ago, when he had come back to the Twin Flame Retreat for her. The actor playing Linen continued to play, and she couldn't help the tears running down her face. She missed Greg so much in that moment that she just couldn't bear it. Four months without his touch was just too long. She waited until the scene was over before going to the producer on the set.

"Hey, Karen?"

The woman looked up and smiled, but then frowned when she saw Violet's face. "Are you okay?" She looked at the piano on the set. "Did we get the scene wrong? I thought it went really well."

Violet smiled and shook her head. "Of course not. It was perfect. But I need to go. I need a few days off."

"Is everything okay?"

Karen's concern was making it hard to maintain her composure. "Yes, I just need, I just need to see..."

Without needing any further explanation, Karen

reached out to touch her arm. "I get it. Go. Come back on Monday."

Violet pulled the producer into a hug. "Thank you."

Before the next scene was ready to go, Violet grabbed her bag and left the set, letting a few people know she was going on the way. When she emerged from the studio, she stood in the rain for a few moments, allowing her tears to be washed away before going to find her car. She pulled her phone out, and saw several messages from Greg. She read them and smiled. She decided she would surprise him.

Without bothering to go back to her apartment for any clothes, Violet chose her home address on her satnav, and then started the engine.

By the time Violet was navigating the familiar track that led to the Retreat, she was almost shaking in anticipation. She parked in one of the visitor spaces, and switched off the engine. The silence and darkness enshrouded her and she smiled. She had never felt more at home anywhere else in the world.

She switched off the satnav, grabbed her bag and got out of her car, closing the door quietly behind her. She walked up the driveway, noticing that the lights were on in Julie and Aragonite's cabin, and smiled. At least she knew Greg would be on his own in the house, as there were no other cars there besides his van.

She had the overwhelming urge to knock on the front door, even though it was her own house. She raised her fist, but before she could make contact with the wood, a sound coming from inside the house stopped her.

It was the Moonlight Sonata. Their song. In a state of disbelief, Violet lowered her hand to the door knob and turned it, pushing the door open slowly. When she saw Greg sat at the dusty and unloved piano, tears began to fall for the second time that day.

She waited patiently until he struck the last note, then spoke.

"That was the best welcome home I've ever had."

Greg spun around at the sound of her voice. "Violet?!" He jumped up and crossed the room in a few short strides, before engulfing her in a bear hug. Violet closed her eyes and breathed in his scent, relishing the feeling of his strong arms gripping her tightly and his heat warming her to her core.

After a few moments, he pulled back a little and leaned down to kiss her. The kiss lasted more than a minute, and Violet felt absolute bliss wash over her, relaxing her whole body.

When he pulled away, Violet opened her eyes and smiled up at him. "How did you know I was coming?"

Greg shook his head. "I didn't. I've been having more visions of Atlantis recently, and this evening I was trying to get some work done but all I could think about was you, and how I used to love watching you play the piano, play our song. And without even thinking about it, I found myself sitting here, playing it. Then you appeared, just like I had conjured you from my memories."

"That's incredible. We were filming the scene today where Linen plays the song, and I just had to come back, I just had to see you, so I asked for a few days off. Luckily the producer, Karen, is pretty cool, and she understood."

Greg's face lit up. "You have a few days? When do you have to be back?"

"Not until next week."

Greg kissed her again. "There's nothing in the diary for this weekend, so it can be just us."

"That sounds amazing. I could do with some peace and quiet!"

"Have you eaten yet?"

Violet shook her head and followed Greg into the lounge. "No, I've been driving since late this afternoon."

"I made curry earlier, do you want some?"

Violet dropped her bag on the sofa, relieved to see that everything still looked the same, still felt like home. "Yes, please, I would love that." She followed Greg to the kitchen, and washed her hands then sat at the breakfast bar while he warmed up some curry for her.

"I still can't believe you're here. It's like I manifested you. It's amazing."

Violet laughed. "The Angels obviously wanted us back in each other's arms tonight."

Greg frowned. "Do you think we're being nudged again?"

Violet waved her hand. "Oh no, it was just a figure of speech. I'm sure they're behaving themselves up there after Starlight warned them not to meddle so much."

"I hope so."

A few minutes later, Greg set a wooden plate full of curry and rice in front of her, and a glass of red wine. He poured one for himself and sat next to her.

Suddenly feeling famished, she tucked in, appreciating a decent home-cooked meal after the many takeaways she had eaten on set over the last few months.

"Good?" Greg asked.

She nodded. "Amazing. Thank you. This was exactly what I needed."

"Oh I get it, you didn't come back to see me, you just wanted me for my cooking."

Violet grinned. "Yep, that's it exactly. Just felt curry deprived."

Greg laughed. "Well I can't be too offended, my curry is pretty amazing."

"It really is."

Violet continued to eat. "Tell me what's been happening," she said, in-between mouthfuls.

"Not much, we did another retreat last weekend, which went well. We had a bit of a tricky participant, she was deep in despair over losing her Flame, and was triggered by everything. Took quite a bit of healing and one to one work for her to be able to participate in any sessions without crying or screaming."

Violet raised an eyebrow. "Yikes, that doesn't sound much fun."

"Lisa handled her perfectly. And by the end of the weekend, she was like a different person. I really think she will be able to focus on her own mission now, build a life of her own without her Flame."

Violet sipped her wine. "That's brilliant. Is Lisa okay? I haven't managed to catch up with her recently."

Greg poured himself some more wine and nodded. "She's good, she went out on a second date with Joseph just last night."

Violet nearly spat her wine out in shock. "Joseph?" she sputtered. "Second date?"

"Oh, yeah, his wife split, ditched him for another guy.

So he asked Lisa out. She resisted at first, still stuck in fear herself. But she gave it a go, and I think it's going quite well. I think they're taking things slowly though."

"Wow. That's... amazing. Wow." Violet couldn't articulate herself any better than that. The wine and food and accumulated sleep deprivation was starting to have an effect on her. She yawned.

"Want to watch a movie?"

Violet nodded. She finished eating while Greg went to set up the movie. She took her plate to the sink and washed it, then poured a little more wine before going upstairs.

She set her wine on the low table, then sat down on the mound of cushions next to Greg.

"What are we watching?" she asked with another yawn.

"It's a new one out, The Lily and the Rose. It got great reviews."

"Sounds cool." Violet snuggled up to Greg's side, and he wrapped his arm around her.

All she remembered before drifting into a deep, blissful sleep was the opening credits.

CHAPTER SEVEN

"She's finally asleep," Tadhg said, as he sat on the edge of the bed, removing his prosthetic. There was no reply from Lily, and he assumed she might have fallen asleep. He slid under the covers and put his arm around her. He felt her shoulder shudder a little, and heard a small gasping noise. Frowning, he turned the light on and leaned over so he could see her face. It was streaked with tears, and red.

"Lily? What's wrong? Are you okay?"

Lily sniffed and bit her lip. She shook her head. Tadhg reached over to her bedside to grab some tissues from the box there and handed them to her. She blew her nose.

"Talk to me, Lily, you're scaring me," Tadhg said gently, fearing the worst.

After a few moments, Lily rolled onto her back and looked over at him. "It was a really hard day at work."

Tadhg waited for a few moments, but there didn't seem to be any further information forthcoming. "What happened?" he prompted.

"They asked me to cover maternity today, and we had

an emergency C-section." She closed her eyes. "We did everything we could, but the baby was stillborn."

Tadhg winced. "Oh Lily, that's awful."

"I know I've seen it all, death, injury, illness, and by now it shouldn't affect me, but, I don't know, it was the parents. They were utterly devastated, and all I could think of was what if that had happened to me? What if we had lost little Hattie? Her birth was far more traumatic, yet somehow she made it. But it could so easily have happened to us." Lily began to sob, and Tadhg pulled her close to him.

"Shh, it's okay. It's okay that it hurts you, it means you have a beautiful heart, and that you empathise with your patients. That's not a bad thing, not at all."

He held Lily as she cried, and his heart swelled up with love, and pride. He was so very proud to be able to call this wonderful woman his wife. She worked so hard saving lives, tending to the sick, and he knew that without her, and without their little girl, he would be lost.

"I love you," he said, kissing Lily on the forehead. "I have no doubt that you did everything possible, but maybe the little soul just needed to go home."

Lily nodded, her sobs beginning to calm a little. She blew her nose once again, and pulled some strands of hair away from her face. "I love you too. I don't know why it hurt me so much. I think it was just seeing the parents holding the little bundle that they wouldn't be taking home with them."

"Do they have any other children? Or was that their first?"

"I think they have a daughter already. I'll see them on my shift tomorrow. The mum will be kept in a few nights.

I just feel so awful for her, even though she'll be in a private room, she's still on the postnatal ward full of new mothers and their babies, without her own baby."

"It is awful," Tadhg agreed. "And I'm so glad you will be there to take care of her."

Lily smiled at him. "You always know the right things to say."

"You taught me well."

Lily laughed, and Tadhg smiled back, pleased that he had been able to break her melancholy. "Shall we get some sleep? she asked.

Tadhg switched the lamp off, and pulled her into his arms. She nestled into him, and sighed softly.

"Goodnight," she whispered.

"Good night, my love. Goodnight."

* * *

"Mum? I'm hungry."

Julie opened one eye and peered at her youngest, who was still sporting a couple of black eyes from his nose-breaking incident.

"What time is it?" Aragonite mumbled, waking up beside her.

Julie opened her other eye and peered at her phone on the shelf beside the bed. "It's 6.30," she replied, a yawn escaping from her lips.

Aragonite groaned and pulled the covers up higher. Julie smiled at Jerry. "Shall we get you some cereal?"

"There isn't any left. That's why I woke you. I think Daniel ate it all again."

This time it was Julie who groaned. "That boy is like a bottomless pit! Okay, honey, I'll go over to Greg's, I'm sure he won't mind if we borrow some cereal. I'll go shopping later, again." She sat up and swung her legs out of bed, then grabbed her fleece jacket and put it on. Jerry went back to the small room he shared with his siblings, and she went to the cabin door, and shoved her sockless feet into her boots. She opened the door and stepped out, shivering in the early morning air.

Despite feeling a little grumpy about being pulled away from her warm bed, Julie smiled as she listened to the birdsong, and watched the sunlight filtering through the trees as she walked to the house. It really was quite difficult to be annoyed in such beautiful surroundings.

She reached the door, and got the key from the hiding place and unlocked it. She slipped off her boots, and as quietly as possible, she entered the house, and headed for the kitchen.

When she saw someone standing by the kettle, she jumped, and let out a tiny shriek.

Violet spun around, and shrieked a little herself.

"Oh my goodness! Violet!" Julie rushed over to the Old Soul, engulfing her in a hug.

Violet laughed, recovering from her shock. "Julie! You made me jump!"

"When did you get back? Has the filming finished? Is everything okay?"

Violet pulled away and got another cup out for her friend. "Last night, and yes, everything is fine. I just needed a break! Filming doesn't finish for another couple of months yet."

"It's so good to see you. Greg has been keeping us updated on what you're up to, but it's weird you not being here for so long. The kids will be excited to see you." She reached for the box of cereal on top of the fridge. "I need to borrow this for the kids. I'll go shopping later to replace it. Don't go anywhere, I'll be back for that cuppa and a catch up!"

Violet nodded and poured their drinks, and Julie quickly took the box of cereal back to the cabin. Once Jerry was happy, she went to her bedroom to tell Aragonite that she was going to be in the house with Violet, but she could hear him snoring gently, and didn't want to disturb him.

She went back to the house, and found Violet sitting at the breakfast bar, drinking a fruit tea. She settled on a stool next to her.

"So tell me all about it! From what Greg was saying, it sounded amazing. I really cannot wait to watch it."

"It is amazing, I mean, it's really hard work. I'm only up so early this morning because this is my normal wake up time now. Sometimes we have to be on set for four or five in the morning. So I've been a bit exhausted. But it's magical. Seeing the characters come to life. Seeing the sets," Violet sipped her tea. "It's really amazing. Especially seeing as the film artist was there too! He was a professor at the Academy."

"No way! That's amazing! Who was he?"

"Suede. The quiet one." Violet smiled. "It shouldn't surprise me anymore, but I'm still amazed every time I meet one of the characters in real life!"

"That's because it's incredible."

Violet nodded. "It really is. I saw my spiritual sisters

recently, I got the evening off, and Maggie had gathered them all together."

"Oh, that's wonderful, how are they all doing?" Julie nabbed a biscuit from the nearby tin, and nibbled on it. Her stomach was beginning to growl.

"They're all really good. All with their Flames, all following their missions, and thanks to adopting our manifestation rituals, they've been manifesting all they need, too."

Julie frowned. "Why does it feel like you're going to say 'but'?"

Violet smiled. "Because, well, it all seems a bit too good to be true? Everyone is healthy, happy, wealthy, and loving their lives? It's not something I've encountered much before!"

Julie laughed. "Yes, it does seem like a foreign concept."

"Maggie had a vision of us all, while I was there. She said we would all be together in the end. I said that was amazing, and that made me happy, but, she didn't look that happy about it."

Julie frowned. "Why not?"

"No idea," Violet replied, shrugging. "She didn't elaborate. Anyway. Are things good with you and Aragonite? And the kids?"

Julie grinned. "Yes, we love our little cabin. Still amazed that Greg and Aragonite built it! The kids still love it here. They are doing really well in school. Though they have been getting up to mischief too!" Julie explained their most recent incidents to Violet, making her laugh.

Julie glanced up at the clock on the wall. "I should get back, the other two will be waking up, and Aragonite will wonder where I've gone."

Violet yawned and nodded. "I might just get back into bed, I'll see you later?"

Julie smiled and hugged the Old Soul. "Yes, later."

She got back to the cabin to hear Charlotte and Jerry shouting at each other and sighed. Not everything in her life was perfect it seemed.

* * *

"What's wrong?"

Aria glanced up at Linen from where she sat on a towel on the beach. The sun was setting over the Pacific Ocean, but despite the beauty of the scene before them, Linen could feel her melancholy.

She patted the space next to her, and he settled down onto it. "Nothing," she said softly, looking back at the giant orange sun, which was getting ready to disappear.

"You know you can't lie to me. There's something wrong, I can feel it." Linen frowned. It wasn't like Aria not to be upfront about her feelings. She always said what was on her mind.

Aria sighed. "I was just thinking about what Shelley said to me, about the plastic in the sea, and about the nuclear waste. And it makes me sad. Did you know there is more plastic than sea life in there?" she asked, waving her hand at the calm water a few feet away. "The oceans are dying. And it makes me wonder if there are any Mermaids left, and if there will be any life left in it at all in just a few years' time."

"There might not be," Linen said softly, his own heart heavy. "But then, according to your memories, none of us will be here in a few years' time. We will all have gone home."

"Yeah, I know. This was just for twenty years, it wasn't going to be forever, but I guess I had still hoped that we could change things. That it could be different. But nothing is changing."

Linen wrapped his arm around Aria as the sun began its final descent, and the temperature began to drop. "That's not totally true. More Flames have reunited this time, more Earth Angels have Awoken. At least, compared to what I can remember."

Aria was quiet for a while, and all Linen could hear was the waves rolling onto the white sand, and her soft sigh.

"I guess I just feel sad today. And I wish that we could have really saved the world, all of us Earth Angels. When I think of all the Faeries who will have lost their homes in the last few years, all so that companies can make junk food with palm oil and sell the latest clothes and gadgets…"

Linen felt her shoulders shudder, and he glanced down to see tears rolling down her cheeks.

"It just doesn't make sense to me, it really doesn't. How can anyone justify it?"

Linen considered her question for a while. When he finally spoke, the sun had disappeared completely, and the stars were beginning to come out. "I guess they just don't know any different. Technology has been evolving and growing over the last four or five decades, and now we can't live without it. Fashion has changed to the point where it is no longer about being practical or sensible or ethical, it's about having the latest designs and trendiest colours. People have been conditioned to think that it's okay to eat meat, dairy, eggs and other animal products, and that it's weird not to, despite what it's doing to the animals or the environment. I guess we can see that it's all wrong because we didn't grow up with it, we entered the world right in the middle of it, and it seems nonsensical to us."

"Like the frog being boiled slowly?"

Linen smiled and reached out to wipe her tears from her cheeks. "Yes. We jumped into the boiling hot water and wonder why there are a bunch of dead frogs at the bottom. We wonder why they didn't jump out. But if they did jump out, the companies would have to take notice and change the way they did things."

Aria smiled too, but it seemed forced.

"Do you wish you hadn't come?" Linen asked. "Do you want to go home?"

Aria was quiet for so long that Linen became afraid of her answer.

"No," she replied eventually. "I've loved every moment here, especially with you. We have seen some incredible places, we've done some amazing things, none of which I'd ever dreamed of doing before. I wouldn't change any of that."

"But now?" Linen prompted.

"No, I don't want to go home, not yet. There are still more places to see. We're heading to California soon, and after learning so much about North America in the Academy, I would like to actually see more of it." She looked up at Linen. "I'll miss it here though. I think out of everywhere we've been so far, Hawaii is my favourite place. I hope we can come back and see Shelley and Angela again one day."

Linen smiled and leaned down to kiss her. "I'm sure we will. Now, can we go back up to the hut?" He shivered. "I'm getting cold."

Aria smiled. "Can we stay here just a few more minutes? I want to see the stars."

"Okay." They lay back on the towel, and Linen wrapped his arms around her, still shivering a little in his shorts and t-shirt. "Just a few more minutes."

CHAPTER EIGHT

"You're going to visit him again?"

Louise frowned at her husband. "Yes. He just lost his son, he's an old friend, and he hasn't got anyone to support him right now. I can't just leave him on his own."

"What about me? Do I deserve to be left on my own while you go and spend time with another man?"

The petulance in her husband's voice made her wince. "You don't seem bothered about being left alone when there's a match on," she said, referring to his sports obsession. "And you haven't just lost someone you loved. Please be patient, this is important to me."

For a moment, her husband's expression softened and Louise thought he might be about to express something other than childishness, but then it hardened again.

"Whatever," he muttered, before stalking off back to the lounge, where he would undoubtedly be watching the sports channel all evening.

Louise took a deep breath, and closed her eyes. She counted to ten, knowing that getting angry at him for being insensitive would not put her in the best frame of mind for being supportive to Oscar. Although Louise knew that her husband had a right to feel annoyed, she also knew that if she had been visiting a female friend, he wouldn't be so angry about it.

She felt a twinge of guilt then. Of course, her husband was also right to feel jealous, because she did still have feelings for Oscar, not that she had told him that.

She sighed and shook her head. She couldn't think about it all now. She picked up her handbag, then took her keys off the hook by the door. She considered calling out to say goodbye, but figured he wouldn't hear her anyway, considering the volume of the TV. She slipped out the front door, and locked it behind her. Once out of the house, she felt free, and excited to be on her way to see Oscar again, even though it was not in the best of circumstances.

She was so used to the route now that the journey went by quickly and Louise was pulling up in front of Oscar's home in what seemed like no time at all.

She turned off the engine and got out of the car. She wondered what she would find this time. On previous visits, she had found Oscar in various stages of distress and anger. The funeral had taken place the day before. Louise had offered to be there, but Oscar hadn't wanted her to come, he said it would just make things awkward with his ex.

She walked up the path, and when she got to the front door, she didn't bother to knock, she just let herself in. Oscar never bothered to lock his front door, and usually just called out to enter whenever she knocked, so she figured it wouldn't be a problem.

She headed towards the light in the living room. When she stepped through the doorway, her eyes widened.

The place was spotless. On previous visits, the place had been a complete mess, and though she had tried to tidy, he'd always stopped her. She looked around the room, impressed.

"Thought it was time to get things in order."

Louise turned to see Oscar coming up behind her, from the kitchen. "It's looking really good. You didn't need to clean on my account," she said playfully, wondering if it was too soon to try making him laugh.

He smiled, but it didn't quite reach his eyes. "James would have been horrified at the mess, he was always such a neat freak."

As he spoke his son's name, his eyes began to well with tears. Louise reached out to touch his arm. "How did the funeral go?"

Oscar shook his head, the tears beginning to fall. Louise reached her arms out around him and pulled him into a hug. "I'm so sorry," she whispered, her own eyes filling with tears. "I wish there was something I could do."

"Just being here," Oscar said, "Means more than you could know."

They hugged for a while, and after a few minutes, Louise felt a deep feeling of bliss wash over her. Though her heart was breaking for Oscar's loss, she knew that she had never felt more at peace or at home than she did in that moment, with his arms wrapped around her waist.

Afraid that he would be aware of her shift, she pulled back. "Shall I put the kettle on?"

Oscar shook his head and wiped his eyes with his sleeve.

"I have some whiskey."

Louise smiled and followed him to the sofa where he poured them both a glass.

When they were both settled next to each other, and Oscar had turned the electric fire on, Louise sipped her whiskey then looked at Oscar. "My husband is starting to get jealous," she said, hoping to changes the subject and lighten the mood a little.

Oscar raised an eyebrow "I'm not surprised. You have been here a lot in the last week."

Louise frowned. "Is it too much? I just thought..."

"No," Oscar said, reaching over to touch her knee. "I appreciate it. I'm just seeing it from your husband's point of view. With you visiting an old flame so much."

Louise made a face and Oscar tilted his head. "He doesn't know? That it's me?"

Louis shook her head. "No, I told him it was an old friend. I didn't specify which one."

Oscar finished his whiskey, then picked up the bottle to pour another one. "Good thing you didn't tell him, otherwise he really would have cause to be jealous."

Louise smiled. "It's not like anything has happened. I just didn't want you to be on your own right now."

"Doesn't mean neither of us has thought about it. Why would you have emailed me otherwise? Why would I have replied?"

Louise's heart started hammering and she downed the rest of her drink, barely noticing the burning liquid making its mark on her throat. "What are you saying?" she whispered, setting her glass down on the coffee table.

Oscar downed his second glass, then moved closer to

her on the sofa. "I'm saying that I still love you. I know it's been a long time, but I love you."

Eyes wide, Louise was at a loss for words. She didn't move as he leaned closer, and tucked a stray strand of hair behind her ear. When his fingers touched her ear, she shivered.

"I've missed you, Louise. From the moment I realised we were Twin Flames, I have kicked myself over and over for ever having let you go."

Louise blinked. "Twin Flames? How did you know that?"

Oscar smiled. "I read a book that made me realise. Called the Earth Angel Academy or something. A friend gave it to me."

Louise swallowed hard. "*The Earth Angel Training Academy.* I read that book too. I even attended a retreat, run by the author."

"You did? So you understand? About Twin Flames?"

Louise nodded, and she began to lean closer to him. When he closed the final few inches, and her lips met his, instead of the fireworks that she had imagined there might be, there was an overwhelming feeling of utter bliss. His kiss deepened and intensified, and Louise felt a stirring in her stomach that she hadn't felt in years. He pulled her closer, and she began to kiss him with more passion and fervour than she had felt in a long time.

Before she could really process what was happening, he was pulling her up off the couch, and he took her by the hand and led her to his bedroom. Despite it feeling wrong to betray her husband, in every other way, it had never felt more right.

They crossed over the threshold, and both began discarding their clothing. At one point, Oscar kissed her then whispered. "We don't have to do this, I don't want you to do anything you will regret."

In response, Louise kissed him back and smiled, burying the guilt in a dark corner. "I want you."

Oscar smiled and led her to the bed. "I was hoping you would say that."

* * *

Violet's few days off went by all too quickly, and suddenly it was Sunday evening. She had to be up early in the morning to be back on set by lunchtime.

"It's been so good to have you back here," Lisa said, passing the bowl of carrots to Violet. Greg had invited them to dinner, along with Julie and Aragonite, and Ruby and her Twin Flame Dylan, so they could see Violet before she had to go back to work.

Violet accepted the carrots with a smile and put some on her plate before passing them to Ruby. "It's been so good to be back. I've really missed you all."

"And the food," Greg added with a grin.

"Oh definitely. Actually I think I missed the food more."

Everyone laughed. Once they all had full plates, they dug in, and Violet glanced up to see Greg staring at her. She smiled, and reached her leg out, until her foot found his under the table. The last few days with him had been exactly what her soul needed. She had been on the edge of burning out, without actually realising it. She was determined to make sure that she didn't exhaust herself during the rest of the filming process.

As her friends chattered and ate around her, Violet breathed in deeply, trying to savour the flavour of the food, and the feelings of peace and joy she was experiencing.

"So when will the movie be out again?"

Violet smiled at Dylan. "They're aiming for the new year I think. I'm not a hundred percent sure yet."

"Have you seen any of it yet? What you've filmed so far?" Ruby asked.

Violet shook her head. "No, I hope to be allowed to see some of the editing process though. And I'm very excited about the score. They've chosen this amazing composer, and I think it will really pull it all together. Although we won't be ready for that part for a while yet."

Lisa shook her head. "It all so amazing, I still remember reading the book, and thinking – this needs to be on the big screen, but for it to actually be happening, it kind of blows my mind a bit."

Violet chuckled. "It blows my mind too, and I'm working on it."

"I always knew it would happen," Greg said.

Violet frowned at him. "Really? How?"

Greg sipped his wine and shrugged. "I don't know. Remember when we were here the first time? And I said I could see you writing a book? Well I could see films, too, but I didn't want to freak you out."

Violet raised an eyebrow. "Oh really?"

Greg nodded. "Yes, I could see it, clear as day. Me and you, on the red carpet, at the premiere."

Realising that he was being serious, and wasn't just teasing her, Violet smiled and rubbed his foot with hers.

"That's amazing. Obviously you will be my plus one to the premiere."

"I better be."

"Julie was saying you've been having other visions, Greg? About Atlantis?"

As Greg started to explain to Aragonite and the others about his Atlantis visions, Violet felt herself fade away from the room, and saw herself standing on the beach, looking out to the water, feeling lost, but not knowing why.

"Don't you think, Violet?"

The sound of her name brought her back to the present, and she brought her forgotten forkful of food to her mouth, and ate it before responding. "About what?"

"About all the Atlanteans that are popping up at the moment. Dylan realised that he is an Atlantean, and then there's Greg, and Joseph and Ben and Nick. And didn't you say that Vivi and Saphron's Flames in Toronto were Atlantean?"

Violet frowned. "And Jack, who's working on the movie. Huh, I hadn't really thought about it. Maybe we should look into that." She sipped her wine. "I could ask Sarah. I haven't had a good catch-up with her in a while. Perhaps Gold knows something."

"Maybe all the Atlantean men need to get together? Perhaps something will come of a face to face meeting?" Julie suggested.

"But Henry and Sam are in Canada. It's a bit of a long way to come just to chat," Violet protested.

"Actually, I received an email from Saphron. I was going to keep it a surprise, but I need to ask you about your filming schedule, so you can be here. They want to visit, to come on a retreat. Apparently Sam has been having visions too."

Violet's eyes widened and she smiled. "Oh, I would love to see Saphron and Vivi again! When are they thinking of visiting?"

"Probably in the autumn, what do you think of an Atlantean Men's Retreat?"

Violet looked at Greg who was nodding slowly. "I think that could be quite powerful," he said. "Just the men though?"

"We had planned to do retreats for men only," Violet reminded him. "I think it's a great idea. I'm sure that Saphron and Vivi and I would be busy chatting, and perhaps we could have our own female gatherings at the same time. In-between feeding you guys, of course."

Julia nodded. "That's settled. I'll start creating the info. Although, we already pretty much have a guest list. I'll work out the costs."

Violet smiled. "Wow, I have to admit, I am so glad that you agreed to do all the admin side while I'm away, you have a knack for it."

"Hey, are you saying I'm no good at it?" Greg protested.

"Of course not, honey," Violet said sweetly. "But you hate computers, and quite honestly, I think they hate you too."

Everyone chuckled, and Greg held his hands up in defeat. "Okay, yeah, you're right. They do." He smiled at Julie. "I'm also really glad that Julie is here. She makes it all work." He looked around the table. "We all do."

As the conversation moved on, Violet's earlier vision of the beach, and the feeling of being lost, returned for a moment, making her frown. She had no idea what it meant, but she imagined it would become clear in time.

* * *

"The Angels told you what?" Astrid asked, her face no doubt giving away her disbelief and amusement.

"That we should move in together. Above the café. I've been considering moving there, as it was about to come up for rent, but I wasn't sure." Xander grabbed a handful of popcorn from the bag she held and munched on them slowly. Their chosen film still played on the screen in front of them, entirely forgotten.

"Are you sure that it's the Angels telling you to ask me to move in? Perhaps you just thought it wouldn't seem so sudden or weird this way?" She watched his face, a smile on her lips. He looked into her eyes, a slightly guilty looking smile on his face.

"Okay, okay, so maybe I asked the Angels if we should, and they just agreed."

Astrid nodded. "That sounds more likely. Well, I think it's a great idea."

"You do?" Xander's mouth dropped open in shock.

Astrid laughed. "Of course I do. I know it's quite quick, and we've only been together a few weeks, but, it feels good when I consider it. I think we would have fun living together. And it would save me all the bus fares to and from the café. I could simply just go downstairs."

She reached out to gently lift Xander's chin and close his mouth. "Why do you disbelieve that I want to be with you so much?" she whispered, kissing him softly on the lips.

Xander kissed her back, then sighed. "I spent so long, trying to accept that we wouldn't be together, that it wasn't the right thing for us, that it's just taking me a while to adjust to it being different. I have asked the Angels why it is different, what changed, and all I got was – it hasn't changed."

Astrid frowned, and her heart skipped. "What do you mean, it hasn't changed?"

"I mean, this was the path they intended for us the whole time. That they only showed me what I needed to see to make sure I did not seek to be with you, because we weren't meant to be together until now."

Louise raised an eyebrow. "Wow, that's a bit manipulative, isn't it? I thought Angels were meant to guide and assist, but not mess with our free will."

"I guess my Angels didn't get that memo," Xander said dryly.

Astrid giggled and kissed him again. She then snuggled into his side, and tried to work out what was happening in the film. They seemed to have missed an important conversation whilst having their own. She thought of them living together, and she smiled to herself. She had never imagined it would be possible, but it was finally happening. She had spoken to Louise the day before, who had confided her infidelity to her. All they needed was for Delia to be reunited with Quentin, and it would be a true Twin Flame miracle, all three women, with their Twin Flames, against all odds.

"What's happening?" Xander whispered, staring at the screen.

"I have no idea," she replied, "shall we rewind a little?"

"Good idea." Xander grabbed the remote and tried to go back to where the film would make sense to them. But Astrid knew she was too lost in her own thoughts to be able to concentrate anyway. It was also difficult to concentrate when she could feel the heat of Xander's body through her clothes, and smell his shampoo. She looked up at him.

"Although..."

"What?"

"Perhaps there's something better we could do," she said with a grin.

CHAPTER NINE

Charlie watched his daughter sleeping, her tiny body rising and falling with each breath, and he couldn't stop the tears from running down his cheeks. He had finally brought Ceri home a few days before, and they had picked Juliet up from Ceri's mother's house.

Even though he had been eager for Juliet to speak before, he had to admit, he was glad that she couldn't. That she couldn't ask him where her little brother was. Why she couldn't meet him.

He did his best to try and explain it to her, but he wasn't sure if it had made any sense. He put her favourite book to one side, and slowly got to his feet, his limbs stiff from sitting on the stool next to her cot.

Charlie left her room, leaving the door ajar, and went downstairs to the lounge. Ceri was watching a movie on the TV, but he could tell from her expression that she wasn't really watching it.

"She's asleep," he whispered, though why he was whispering, he had no idea.

"That's good," Ceri replied, her voice devoid of emotion. "Movie any good?"

Ceri shrugged. "I have no idea."

Charlie reached for the remote and hit the pause button. "Are you okay?"

Ceri looked at him, unshed tears in her already bloodshot eyes. "I don't think I'll ever be okay again," she whispered. "I don't know how to deal with this. How to carry on when right now I should be feeding and changing my little boy."

Charlie sighed. "I know, it's going to take some time, to… accept it. To get used to it. But we need to carry on, for Juliet's sake. We're still a family."

Ceri nodded, her tears spilling over. "I know. But, I can't just yet."

Charlie put his arm around his wife and rested his cheek on her head. "Take all the time you need. I'm here, I can do everything for Juliet. I spoke to work, and they're still giving me the paternity leave, so you don't have to do anything for a couple of weeks."

He could feel her shoulders shaking, and his own eyes filled with tears. Despite his strong words, he also wanted to curl up in a ball and do nothing, the pain of losing his perfect son was too much to bear.

And they still had to plan the funeral. They still needed to bury their baby. But he couldn't even comprehend thinking about it right in that moment. It was too much.

He pressed the play button on the remote, and decided to lose himself in a fictional story, because it was easier than feeling the pain stuck in his chest.

* * *

"It's all booked!"

Sam looked up to where Saphron stood in the door of his workshop. "What is?"

"Our trip to the UK! I spoke with Julie, and they're even running a special retreat for only a few specific people while we're there."

Sam set his tools down. "Oh? What kind of retreat will it be?"

"A men's only retreat for Atlanteans! Vivi and Henry are booking their flights and everything right now." Saphron was so excited, she was bouncing up and down. She couldn't wait to see her friend again, and to finally meet Greg.

"I'm confused, men only? What about you and Vivi?" Sam asked.

"Oh, we women will be doing our own thing, I'm sure. We have so much to catch up on."

"Okay, well, when are we going?"

"First weekend of October. They said it was okay to arrive a day early, to give us a chance to adjust, and we can stay a couple of days after. Then I've booked for us to see a few sights in London. You know I've been itching to sightsee there."

"How long in total? I'll need to book time off work."

"Two weeks, I've printed everything out and left it on your desk."

Sam came over to her and kissed her. "Thank you. That makes it much easier for me."

"I know, that's why I did it," Saphron teased. "I need to figure out what to pack!" She left the workshop, and headed back to the house, undeterred when Sam called out after her.

"But it's weeks away yet!"

Honestly, he'd probably pack the day before they leave. But she needed to make sure she had the right things to take, she had a feeling it was going to be a life-changing trip.

* * *

"Robert! Oh my goodness, it's so good to see you!" Violet said, wrapping her arms around her American friend. He had contacted her the day before and asked if he could visit her on set. "Hope the trip from London wasn't too bad. What brings you here? How's your wife? Can I get you a drink?"

Robert chuckled. "Yes, I'll take that drink. The trip was fine, smooth as. Wife is brilliant, she says hi." He accepted the iced lemonade she offered him, then sat down on the sofa seat in her little trailer. She sat opposite him.

"As for why I'm here, honestly, I'm here to thank you."

Violet frowned. "You came all the way from Arizona to the UK to thank me?"

Robert laughed. "Well, no, from London. I was here anyway, promoting my new book. But when I realised you were so close, I needed to see you."

Violet shook her head. "I'm confused, what did I do?"

"You told me about Kasey."

"Kasey? The healer?" Violet smiled. "You've met her then?"

Robert nodded slowly. "Yes. She was in Arizona, and I just knew I had to go. She knew who I was immediately, I don't know how. But then she sat with me, and then hugged me, and that was a year ago."

"Oh, I'm so glad you two got to meet. We meant to do something together, but then this film happened and we never managed to connect again." Violet sipped her lemonade. "I'm still not sure why you needed to thank me though?"

"Because I am healthy. Completely, one hundred percent, not a thing wrong with me, healthy."

Violet put her drink down, her eyes wide. "You mean, she healed you?"

Robert nodded. "When I met her I could feel I was close to the end. The Angels were beginning to call me, I could almost hear them. But then she took me in her arms, and whispered to me – 'It's not time yet, we need you here.'" His eyes welled up. "I didn't even realise until a month later that all my pain had gone. That I no longer ached. My stomach was settled. And I had energy." He shook his head. "I went to the doctors, and they did all the tests. I'm clear, completely clear."

Tears were running down Violet's cheeks freely, and she leaned across the tiny space to hug her friend. "Oh Robert, that really is the most amazing news I have heard in so long. I am so, so happy for you, honestly, I cannot tell you how happy I am."

"Thank you. For caring so much, for telling me to meet Kasey. For everything."

"Anytime, my beautiful friend. Anytime."

"I love you," Robert whispered into her ear. "You're my angel."

Violet smiled and hugged him a little tighter. "I love you too, beautiful soul." After a while she pulled back and grabbed a tissue to wipe her face, and offered one to him. "Now then, how about we take a tour of the set? We're filming some pretty fun scenes today."

Robert blew his nose and nodded. "Sounds good to me. Lead the way."

* * *

"So we have seven men confirmed for the retreat so far," Julie said to Greg, while he stirred the soup he was making for them all. "Henry, Sam, Ben, Joseph, Nick, Jack and Dylan. With their contributions, costs should be covered, and we have enough accommodation for them all. Only Saphron and Vivi will be extras, but Violet said they would be her guests?"

Greg put a lid on the pot and nodded. "Yes, they will. That's great, so they've all booked in and paid? They were all available and wanted to come?"

"Yes," Julie said, making some notes on her diary. "They were all really excited. I think we should have some meetings with Lisa and Amy, to see what kind of schedule we'll have for the weekend. I'm assuming you'll be running the workshops? You don't want us to do any? I figured we'd just being helping, cooking, cleaning and that kind of thing."

"Yes, that sounds good, though I would appreciate ideas on the workshop content. Lisa was in Atlantis with us, so she may have some thoughts. Although I get the feeling that when we all come together in the same room, we will figure out what needs to happen."

"You think there will be some kind of spark? A recognition?"

"Possibly." Greg poured himself some wine, and waved the bottle at Julie, but she shook her head. He poured her a glass of water instead.

"It will be quite interesting to see the energy created by you all being in the same room as each other," Julie mused, making further notes to herself on things she needed to do when she was back on the laptop.

"Yeah, I feel like we've all been having these visions for a reason. Perhaps it will become clear why when we get together."

"Perhaps what will become clear?" Aragonite asked as he walked into the kitchen.

Greg poured him some wine and explained what he and Julie were discussing.

"Ah, yeah. The Atlantis visions."

"Was it ever mentioned in the Angelic Realm?" Julie asked him as he settled on a bar stool next to her. "Atlantis?"

Aragonite nodded. "Yes, it was, but not in any detail that would help you guys, I don't think. And I haven't had a clear line of communication with Mica or Emerald since I got here. I can only assume they're still running the show up there, but I don't know."

"Do you think they're still nudging people?" Greg asked, a frown on his face.

"I don't think so, I think they've scaled that back now. Instead, Starlight asked them to look for patterns, and only nudge when it didn't interfere with the free will of that person."

"Hmm," Greg said. "How do they know it's not interfering with their free will?"

Aragonite sighed. "The Angels are pretty perceptive.

Before, they could tell they were pushing people in a different direction to what they would choose for themselves. So they should be able to discern what would conflict with their free will or not."

"Are you and Violet having trouble again?" Julie asked, her heart sinking at the thought.

Greg shook his head and switched off the burner underneath the soup. "No, everything's really good. I just get a bit angry when I think of what they did, that's all."

"Maybe you should ask Lisa if you can have a healing session on that," Julie suggested, getting up to get bowls and spoons out. "It would be a good idea to clear that trigger."

Greg acknowledged what she said, but didn't say anything further. Julie set the tables in the front room, then called for the kids to come downstairs, from where they were watching a movie in the workshop room.

They all sat down to eat, and Julie savoured the soup and the homemade garlic bread. She looked around the table at her family and Greg, and gave thanks to the Angels, for surrounding her with such beautiful souls.

"So, when is this retreat happening?" Aragonite asked.

CHAPTER TEN

"Did you hear? They're predicting snow! Snow! In September! How crazy is that?"

Chad looked up at Helen, who was holding their youngest, Ivy, on her hip. He frowned. "That is quite unusual, but, I have to say, considering all the research I've been doing, it doesn't surprise me."

Sensing the seriousness in his tone, Helen held up a hand, then went to the other room to set Ivy down in the lounge with her favourite toys, then she returned to where Chad sat at his desk in his study.

"What research? What's happening?"

Chad sighed. "I took a few classes in college on Environmental Studies, and though I don't use it in any professional capacity, it's remained something of a hobby. I've been tracking and recording all the major natural disasters that have occurred for the last ten years. Earthquakes, hurricanes, volcano eruptions, monsoons, tornadoes, etcetera."

Helen's throat tightened at the mention of earthquakes.

"It does seem like there've been a lot of big disasters in recent years. I guess part of me blocks it out, ever since the quake in Nepal. Her eyes filled with tears. "I don't think I've really gotten over it yet."

Chad stood up and pulled her into a hug. Her tears fell and soaked into his t-shirt. "I don't think I have, either. I miss Todd so much, but I know he's still with me, I can sense him."

Helen nodded into his shoulder. "I don't know what I would have done if it weren't for his sacrifice. He was an amazing soul."

"Yes he was."

They hugged for a few minutes, Helen was listening out for their two kids, aware that they might be causing havoc in the other room.

She pulled away when her tears slowed up. "So what is this pattern? What's happening?"

Chad went over to his desk and held up a chart he had been working on. Helen followed him, and stared at the chart, with symbols and colours and things written on it. It made absolutely no sense to her at all.

"What does it mean?" She asked.

"In a nutshell, weather patterns are getting more extreme. The world is experiencing a record number of hurricanes, with record breaking intensity. The monsoons are the worst we've seen in decades, there are more big storms, there's more extremes across the board, and the seas are rising and increasing in temperature."

"In a smaller nutshell?"

"At some point soon, these natural disasters are going to get so intense, that there will be a mass depopulation, all over the world. Most coastal areas will go under water. Islands may disappear completely." Chad looked up at Helen. "It's not good. I've been thinking that we should sell this place now, and move to higher ground. Get somewhere where we can grow our own food, and become a little more self-sufficient. If we act now, when things get crazy, we will be a little safer."

Helen's eyes widened. "When is this all going to happen?"

Chad looked at his charts, and shrugged. "In the next ten to twenty years is my best guess."

"Shit," Helen breathed. "I've seen so many movies about this, about climate change and weather patterns and the world going into an ice age and all sorts, but I never thought I would live to see it actually happen."

"Me neither. But I think the movies have actually been warnings to us, for quite some time. These extreme weather patterns are not natural. We humans have created them. Blindly thinking that we could overcome whatever was thrown at us. But we're no match for tsunamis and hurricanes."

"Should we tell anyone? Warn them?"

"You could tell any friends living near the coast, or who might be affected, but there's no point in panicking people. I'm sure that there are plenty of scientists who have already figured out what I just have, and besides, I have no real qualifications in this, I don't think anyone would really listen to me."

"Most of my friends live inland, or high up."

Chad nodded. "Like I said, tell who you think might listen and heed your advice without going deep into fear mode, because that's really not very helpful."

"So we need to move?"

"I think it would be wise. If we do it now, we can make sure we're prepared."

Helen looked toward the lounge where their two children played, completely unaware of their discussion. "It feels awful to think that by the time they are teenagers or young adults, that the world might look completely different to what it does now."

"I know. It hurts to think they might never get to experience some of the beautiful places we have seen. But I will do everything I can to make sure they are safe, and they actually get the chance to grow up."

Helen nodded, her eyes filling with tears again. "I know you will."

* * *

"And cut! That's a wrap everyone! Well done!"

A cheer erupted around Violet, and she stood up from her chair to hug the producer and the director and pretty much everyone within reach. They had done it. They had filmed *The Earth Angel Training Academy*. It had taken seven gruelling months, but every scene they wanted had been shot, and now it was down to the post production team to turn it into a finished film.

Violet took the glass of champagne she was offered, and raised her glass to the toast the director made. Although she was happy and relieved that the filming was finally done, she felt a little bit sad too. She had really enjoyed the whole process, and had gotten involved in as many aspects of it as she could. She was going to miss the crew, and the cast, they had begun to feel like a family to her.

When all the festivities died down, the crew began breaking down the sets, and costume staff were running about, gathering their items and the props people were doing the same.

Violet gathered her things, and while no one was looking, she took a small memento from the set, sure that no one would notice it was missing. She was having a meal with the crew that evening, then she was going back to the apartment, sleeping until she felt human again, and then she was getting into her car and going home to her Flame.

Her heart fluttered in her chest at the thought of him. They had finished a few days earlier than scheduled, so she would be able to surprise him again. She couldn't wait.

When she got back to her apartment, she dumped everything on the sofa, then went and stripped off to have a hot shower.

The hot water streaming down her body was exactly what she needed to feel refreshed enough to be sociable all evening. She went into the bedroom, just wrapped in a towel, and picked up her phone from her bag. She had been so busy she hadn't even looked at it all day.

There was a missed call from Sarah and she smiled. She had only been thinking that she hadn't had a chance to speak to her. Deciding there was no time like the present, she hit the button to call her, figuring she could get ready while catching up with her sister.

"Violet! How are things? The Angels were yelling at me to call you, so I thought I better had, is everything okay?"

Violet smiled and perused the few clothes hanging in

her wardrobe. "I'm good, everything's great. I'm just getting ready to go out for dinner with the crew. How are you? How's Gold and the kids?"

"We're all good here, yeah, we've had some ups and downs, but I think things are picking up now."

"Oh good. I've been wanting to speak to you actually, which is probably why you felt the need to call."

"Oh? Tell me more."

While Violet got dressed and applied some makeup, she explained to Sarah about the Atlantean men all having visions and dreams, and how they were holding a retreat just for them, to see if they could figure out what was happening. "So do you or Gold have any ideas? Why this is all coming about now?"

"Huh, I don't think so, I mean, I'll ask Gold, but I haven't heard anything about the Atlanteans and their visions from the Angels."

"You've spoken to Pearl recently? Or Emerald and Mica?"

"Yes, well, a few times during my dreams. They have just said that all is okay there, and that they are continuing to bring people together when they need to be. But perhaps they are behind it, and just haven't mentioned it. Do you know what it's all about?"

"No," Violet said, putting on a hint of mascara. "That's why I thought I'd ask you. I have no idea. Oh well, the retreat is in three weeks, I guess we might find out then."

"Hopefully. You'll have to let me know what they manage to discover."

"I will." Violet glanced at the clock on the bedside table. "I'd better go, our reservations are for eight, and I need to dry my hair."

"Have fun, I love you, sister."

"Love you too," Violet replied before hanging up. She stared at her reflection for a moment. "I wonder what we will discover?" she asked her mirror image.

* * *

Louise's hands were shaking as she posted her keys to the house through the letter box. Oscar was waiting in the van, which was now full of all her possessions.

She had intended to tell her husband, but she couldn't bear to see the look in his eyes. So she had opted to take the coward's way out. She had written him a letter, and left it on the kitchen table.

He must know that things aren't right, Louise tried to convince herself as she walked down the path to the van. *He's not stupid.* She opened the door and slid into the passenger seat, and Oscar reached over to touch her leg.

"You okay?"

She nodded. "Yes. I feel bad for not telling him, but then, I know he wouldn't take it very well. It's better this way."

Oscar looked as unconvinced as she felt, but nodded anyway, then turned the engine on and pulled away from the curb.

They didn't speak on the journey. Louise's mind was in turmoil. She felt so happy to be with Oscar, so relieved that she didn't have to lie to her husband anymore, or pretend everything was okay. But she felt sad too, for the loss of her marriage, and of her old way of life. She knew that she would be much happier with Oscar, but she still felt guilty for how their relationship came about.

She had never imagined she would be the kind of person to have an affair.

When they pulled up in front of his humble home, darkness had fallen. Oscar parked the van and switched off the engine. He smiled at Louise.

"Let's get it all unpacked quickly, and I'll order a pizza to celebrate?"

Louise smiled back. "Sounds brilliant. I'm famished."

Oscar got out of the van, and went to open the door while Louise got out and opened the side door. She breathed deeply, and found some energy from deep within, to start unloading her belongings into her new home.

Only an hour and a half later, the two of them were sat on the sofa, the pizza box half empty on the coffee table, and a fire crackling merrily in the hearth.

"How do you think he took it?" Oscar asked, tucking into another slice.

Louise sighed. She had been wondering the same thing, and wondered if it had been apparent on her face. "Not well, I shouldn't think." She picked up her handbag from the floor and dug around for her phone. There was a text message waiting. She opened it and read it, then looked up at Oscar.

"Well?" he asked.

"It just says 'Goodbye'," Louise replied, her eyes beginning to fill with tears. "Perhaps he took it better than I imagined."

Oscar took her hand in his. "Perhaps he could feel that you had already left him in spirit, and he was expecting it."

"Perhaps." Louise switched her phone off and put it back in her bag. Until they had to deal with getting divorced, she wanted to avoid having to communicate with her husband if possible. She was ready to begin a new life with her Flame.

"Would you like the last slice?" Oscar asked.

She smiled. "Why, yes, I think I would. Thank you." She picked up the remaining slice from the box, and took a bite. The cheese was still warm and gooey.

"James always had to have the last slice."

Louise heart thudded. "I would have given it to him," she said softly, unsure how to react. It was the first time Oscar had uttered his son's name since the funeral.

"He would have taken it, too," Oscar said with a chuckle. "No shame when it came to pizza."

Louise smiled and squeezed his hand.

"He would have loved you," Oscar continued. "I wish you could have met him."

"Me too," Louise said. "Me too."

* * *

"Violet and Greg are holding a retreat for a select group of men."

Steve looked up from the book he was reading. "Oh? A Twin Flame one?"

"No," Maggie said, scanning the email. "It's one for Atlanteans. She was emailing to see if I might run one of the workshops, but I think actually, you need to be there."

"Me? Oh, because you think I was in Atlantis too?"

Maggie smiled at her Flame. "Yes, and not only were you there too, but you were pretty important too."

Steve shrugged. "I wouldn't mind a weekend in the woods. When is it?"

"First weekend of October. Will be lovely colours around then. Shall I reply and ask if we can both be there?"

"Will you do a workshop?"

Maggie frowned. "It doesn't feel like that will be my purpose there, but I would be happy to lead a meditation if the need arrives."

She moved to type a reply, and suddenly the computer and her living room disappeared, and she found herself sitting in a circle of men, in the candlelight.

"I can't believe it. Are you sure? It was our fault?"

One of the men sighed. "It's true. It was all our fault."

"Maggie?"

Maggie blinked and found herself back in her living room again. Steve was calling her.

"Yes? Sorry, I was just,"

"Having a vision? Sorry, I didn't see the look on your face until I'd already said your name. Just wanted to know if you wanted a cuppa."

Maggie smiled. "Yes, please." She typed out a quick reply to Julie's email, and tried to shake off the lingering feeling of foreboding from her vision.

CHAPTER ELEVEN

"Joseph! Wake up!"

Lisa shook her Flame's shoulders, trying to wake him from the deep slumber where he appeared to be having a nightmare. Finally, his eyes shot open and he gasped.

"It's okay, you're okay, you're safe," she said quickly, trying to calm him down.

When his breathing had slowed a little, she wrapped her arms around him. "What was it? What were you dreaming?"

"I was in Atlantis again," he whispered.

Lisa pulled back and looked at him. "Atlantis? But life there was calm..." She raised an eyebrow. "Were you dreaming of... the end?" she whispered, her heart hammering loudly in her chest.

Joseph nodded. "Yes. Most had left for the seas, but I remained. I had made my wife leave, and I think that's why she never forgave me, even in this life."

"I didn't realise you had stayed. But that would explain why we never found each other again." Lisa sat up against the headboard, and Joseph pulled himself up into a sitting position too. The dim glow of the bedside lamp created bizarre shadows on her bedroom ceiling, as Lisa ran through the memories that had surfaced from their lives in Atlantis.

"I don't know why I stayed," Joseph said. "But in the dream it seemed important. I think a few of us had remained, and we were there when... it was destroyed."

Lisa leaned her head on his shoulder. "I only vaguely remember the ripples through the water, the waves of energy from the destruction. I remember being distraught at the loss of our beautiful city. But then, I don't know, time took on a strange quality under the water. I know we lived there for many centuries, for some reason our transformations into sea-folk rendered us incapable of aging. I guess it took care of the fact that we were unable to reproduce."

"I hadn't really thought about that." Joseph admitted. "Centuries? Really?"

Lisa nodded. "By the time I went home to the other side, and was reincarnated, the world was unrecognisable to me. It could have been another planet. It was nothing like Atlantis."

"What do you think will happen when we all come together again? All the Atlanteans?"

Lisa frowned. "I don't know. But I do hope it helps to stop these nightmares. Maybe it will become clear what really happened back then, and it will clear the air. Maybe it will cause a shift to happen now." She shrugged and yawned. "I guess we'll just have to wait and see."

Joseph turned and kissed her slowly, and despite her tiredness, she felt a stirring within. She didn't resist when his kisses became more passionate, and all thoughts of Atlantis drifted away.

* * *

"Oh Linen, we must go, they need help there, desperately."

Linen felt his resolve melting under his Flame's gaze. "I have no doubt they do, but I haven't been paid for my last lot of travel articles yet, and we are dangerously low on funds ourselves. By the time we pay for flights there, it may be a while before we can afford to leave." He raised an eyebrow. "Do you really want to be stuck on an island with no power or food? We'd end up becoming part of the problem."

Aria sighed. Linen hated to see disappointment on her face, but one of them had to be sensible sometimes.

"I'm sure there are many agencies sending aid, why don't we enquire to see if they need volunteers? Perhaps we could get transport there cheaper?" Linen suggested.

Aria's face brightened up immediately. "Great idea, Lin! I'll get straight on it." She kissed him quickly, then went off to the computer in the tiny room they'd been renting in California since they'd left Hawaii.

Pleased that she was happy again, Linen retrieved his book from the bedside, then headed out to the pool in the complex. He settled into a lounger that was in the shade, and turned to the dog eared page where he'd left off the night before.

After a few pages, however, he realised that he wasn't really taking in the story, and in fact couldn't recall what had happened with the characters at all. He set the book down on the ground and closed his eyes. He was so tired. He knew that Aria thrived on the travelling, on meeting new people, on helping others in need, and he had been enjoying it too. But in that moment, he couldn't stop himself from fantasising about staying in one place for more than a few weeks. Somewhere that was theirs, that they loved, where they could actually relax and have fun. They'd been living out of their rucksacks for years, and it was beginning to wear him down.

"Linen! I've found the perfect organisation! They can get us to the island. We just need to get ourselves to Atlanta! How awesome is that?"

Linen opened his eyes and looked up at his Flame bouncing up and down on her tip toes in excitement. Feeling he had nothing to lose (though he might invoke the wrath of a disgruntled Faerie) he sat up and swivelled his legs around, resting his feet on the ground.

"Okay, I will go with you to help people who have lost everything because of the hurricane on one condition."

Aria's eyes widened and her mouth fell open. "Oh?" she squeaked.

"I want to go home after that."

Aria's eyes grew wider still. "Home? To the Other Side? You want to die?"

Linen chuckled and stood up to hug his Flame. "No, silly. Home to the UK. I want to live in one place for a while. I'm tired of travelling around so much."

He felt her shoulders relax. "Ohhh," she said. "Thank goodness. I thought you were checking out on me." She pulled back and grinned up at him. "Of course we can go home after. I don't mind it there, the weather is a bit sucky, and the people are a bit miserable, but it's not too bad."

Linen chuckled again. "Okay, it's settled then. When do

we leave for Atlanta?"

"Tomorrow?" Aria said, partly asking, partly telling him.

Linen shook his head. "Okay, go book the flights. My card is in my wallet."

"Thank you!" Aria kissed him, then danced away, back to their room.

Linen sat back down on his lounger, which was now in the sun, and lay back, closing his eyes again. He figured he should rest as much as possible. Judging by the images they'd seen on the news, the next few days and weeks could be tough ones.

* * *

"I'm so excited for this retreat," Julie said to Aragonite as they stacked the firewood that Greg and Aragonite had cut up the day before. "It feels like it will be really powerful, having so many Atlanteans all in the same place!"

"Mmmmhmmm," Aragonite mumbled, as he took the logs she offered him and stacked them neatly.

"You don't think so?" Julie asked, trying to decipher his lacklustre response to her enthusiasm.

Aragonite sighed. "I just have a strange feeling about it, that's all."

"Strange?" Julie said, frowning. "In what way?"

Aragonite glanced around to check that they were alone, and lowered his voice. "I think something will be discovered, that may be of detriment to those in the group. And I don't know if it will then have a detrimental ripple effect on our current reality, once it is realised."

"It feels like you know more about this than you have let on. What could they possibly discover that would have such an awful effect?"

Aragonite shook his head. "That's just it. I don't know any details. Honestly. It's just this feeling I have that I can't seem to shake."

Julie could sense the truth in his words. But it frustrated her. Now, instead of feeling excited about the retreat she too felt a sense of foreboding. "Should we warn Greg? That something bad might happen?"

"So he can be stressed out about it too? No, let's not mention this to anyone. Running the retreats is stressful enough without vague bad feelings being added to the mix."

Julie sighed and continued handing him the logs. "I kind of wish you hadn't told me now."

"Sorry." Aragonite leaned over to kiss her. "I will keep my weird premonitions to myself in future."

"Don't be silly," Julie said with a smile. "I'm glad you can share your thoughts and feelings with me." She tilted her head to one side as a thought suddenly occurred to her. "What if we set the intention to change that? To change whatever the bad thing was going to be? Surely the Angels can do something about it?"

Aragonite had his back to her, but she saw in his posture that what she had said wouldn't be possible. "Sure," he said, turning around to her, but not meeting her eyes. "Let's ask the Angels to do something."

Julie smiled and nodded, but knew that he was just trying to make her feel better. Regardless, she spent the rest of the afternoon, praying to the Angels that the retreat would go well and that Aragonite's feelings of doom would be unfounded.

* * *

"Only two weeks to go! Are you excited? I have been driving Henry crazy! I've been researching all the places we absolutely have to visit. Please tell me you want to go to Glastonbury and Stonehenge, because they are the top two on my list."

Saphron grinned at her friend while she chopped up a head of lettuce. "Oh absolutely. We have to visit those places. I'm so glad that Sam has agreed to drive a rental car, it will make it so much easier to see things. I think the Retreat would be quite tricky to get to with public transport too."

Vivi stroked Angel, and the fluffy cat purred under her touch. "Definitely. Driving will make it easier. Though I don't relish the idea of being on the other side of the road! I might just have to close my eyes."

Saphron chuckled. "Me too. I mean, I trust Sam's driving but it is a scary idea. Especially as we'll be driving from London."

"Have you spoken to Violet? Is everything ready?"

Saphron put the lettuce in the bowl and started on the cucumber. "Yes, I spoke to her online last night. She's happy to have finally finished filming, though apparently will need to go back for some reshoots next month. They've been busy getting everything ready for the retreat. All of the Atlanteans they know will be there. Well, the men, anyway."

"It gives me the shivers thinking of the power the retreat will have. I mean, they were the inventors, the creators.

Violet told us about what they managed to manifest as a group, with only a few Atlanteans present. Can you imagine what this group could manifest? Amazing."

"I'll certainly be interested to see what happens," Saphron agreed as she put the bowl of salad on the table. "Sam has been quite preoccupied recently, I think he can sense that something big is about to happen."

"Big in a good way?"

Saphron sat next to Vivi and reached out to stroke Angel's soft fur. "I'm not sure," she said, her voice lowered. "My gut tells me that it's not good. But that it's necessary. Whatever that means."

Vivi frowned too. "Huh, well I'm sure we will have a good time anyway. I've never been to England before!"

Saphron got up and continued to prepare their meal. "Me neither. What were the other places you wanted to visit while we're there?"

* * *

"Hey gorgeous, what are you up to?"

Tadhg looked up from his laptop at Lily, who had just arrived home after a twelve hour shift. She looked exhausted. He closed the laptop and got to his feet, feeling stiff from having sat still for so long.

"Oh, just some research. Can I get you a drink? I'll heat your dinner up if you're hungry too."

"I'm famished," Lily said with a yawn. "Dinner and a glass of wine sounds amazing." She kissed Tadhg as he passed her on the way to the kitchen, then shrugged off her coat and flopped into a chair.

"Busy shift?" Tadhg asked, switching on the oven and then pulling a bottle of white wine from the fridge.

"Yeah, usual stuff. Although this ward is actually making me miss the maternity ward."

"It's worse than screaming mothers and babies? Wow, must be bad," Tadhg commented, handing her the glass of wine before returning to put her dinner in the oven to heat up.

"It just feels like things are getting more hectic every day, we literally have no time to even fill out our notes in-between patients, let alone pee or eat or take a deep breath."

Tadhg joined her back in the lounge with his own glass of wine. "They do seem to be perpetually understaffed. It's not fair on you, you work long hours and those hours are filled to the brim. It's crazy."

Lily took a sip of wine and nodded. "I can't see it changing any time soon though, it's just the way it is."

"What if I were earning?" Tadhg asked. "Then you could work less shifts, be home more to spend time with Hattie."

Lily frowned. "We've talked about this though, it's not worth you working and losing your benefits, and we'd end up spending way more on childcare."

"That was only if I was earning the minimum, if I was earning a decent wage, it would work out better."

"Okay, so what amazing job to you have in mind?"

Tadhg set his wine glass down on the coffee table and reached for his laptop. Then he turned the screen toward Lily. She leaned forward and read the words on the screen. She turned to him, perplexed.

"You want to become a motivational speaker?"

Tadhg could hear the incredulity in her voice, and he

did his best not to feel hurt by it. "Yes. Do you think it's a terrible idea? Only this charity is specifically looking for people who have lost limbs, who can talk to others in a similar situation, and also to large groups of people who don't understand what it's like to lose a part of yourself."

"But," Lily said, frowning. "What would you talk about? How you lost your leg in a road rage fuelled RTA? Then proceeded to spend months locked away by yourself?"

Tadhg could feel his frustration rising up, and he took a deep breath to remain calm. His nose alerted him to Lily's dinner in the oven, and he set his laptop back down and went to rescue it before it burned.

"I know that it might not seem like my story is very inspiring, but I think that's why it's perfect. I was, and am, a perfectly ordinary guy. I didn't suddenly want to become a Paralympian, or to overcome my disability in some heroic way. I reacted the way that most ordinary people would, and yet I have still managed to marry the most beautiful woman," he said, smiling as he placed the dinner tray on Lily's lap. "And become a father to the most gorgeous little girl, and live a pretty normal life. Sometimes, people don't want to hear from superheroes, sometimes, they want to hear from ordinary people, living normal lives, like me."

Lily picked up her fork and dug in. After a couple of mouthfuls, she turned to Tadhg who was sat beside her again. "I'm sold, when do you start?"

Tadhg grinned, and happiness bubbled up, replacing the frustration. "I have to apply, then wait to hear. The speaking fees are pretty good, and should equate to a decent salary, even without all my benefits. And it's not like I wouldn't be able to still take care of Hattie, it's not a full-time job. It might mean travelling a bit though."

"It sounds like you've got it all figured out. And I think you'd be brilliant at it. I'm sorry if I sounded like I doubted you to begin with, it was just a bit of a shock."

Tadhg chuckled. "It certainly isn't what I ever imagined myself doing either, I must admit. But it feels like I need to do something, and if I can help someone who is going through what I did, to see that there is light at the end of the tunnel, then I think that would feel good."

"I think you're right." Lily held out her empty glass. "May I have some more wine, Mr Motivational Speaker?"

Tadhg took the empty glass from her with a smile. "Yes you may, my beautiful wife."

CHAPTER TWELVE

"Violet? Violet, what is it?"

Violet opened her eyes and gasped. She looked over at Greg, who was watching her, concern etched on his face. She reached up to touch her cheek, which was wet with her tears.

"It was just a dream," she said, her voice catching a little with the emotion that was still overwhelming her.

"What was the dream? You were thrashing about and you cried out in your sleep," Greg said, frowning.

"Oh, did I?" Violet closed her eyes and ran over the details she could remember. The dream was slipping from her consciousness. "I was on the beach, in Atlantis, and I could feel something shifting, and changing, a dark presence, that threatened our existence. Then I was in my bed, there, with you, and I had the most terrible vision in my dreams, of the end of our world." She opened her eyes and looked at Greg. "I get the feeling it was more of a memory than a dream. It was very real."

Greg sighed. "Do you think these visions, these

memories, are resurfacing because of this retreat we are about to do? Everyone will be arriving later. Are we just opening a giant can of worms with this?"

Violet shrugged. "I honestly don't know. But the fact that we have all been having these dreams, or these memories or whatever, makes me think that we are doing the exact right thing in bringing everyone together. We need to know what it means, perhaps there is something that we need to heal."

"I'm sure you're right," Greg said, leaning over to kiss her. "I just hope that we can heal it."

Violet's stomach growled and she grinned. "Can we have breakfast before we heal it?"

Greg chuckled. "Sure." He pulled the covers back and sat up. "What do you fancy?"

Violet sat up and wrapped her arms around him. "Actually, to begin with, I quite fancy you."

Greg smiled at her. "In that case..."

By the time they finally emerged to have breakfast an hour later, Violet's stomach was really growling, and there was a loud knocking at the door.

"I'll get the door, you get the kettle on," Violet said, throwing her dressing gown on.

She went downstairs and unlocked the door, and opened it to see Lisa and Joseph stood there.

"Hey, you two, come on in. You do know where the spare key is though, why not just let yourself in?"

"That's what I said," Lisa said, crossing the threshold. "But Joseph insisted on knocking, said it felt rude to come into your home when we might be interrupting something."

Violet chuckled and stepped aside for Joseph to enter as well.

"Was I wrong?" he asked with a smile.

Violet shook her head. "No, you were right, but it's okay, we needed to get up anyway, my stomach is growling, I'm starved!"

She led the way to the kitchen where Greg had the kettle on, and was already making pancake batter. She grabbed a banana and peeled it, biting into it hungrily.

Lisa and Joseph took up their usual places at the breakfast bar. "So is everything ready to go?" Lisa asked. "Do you need us to do anything?"

Violet swallowed her mouthful and nodded. "Mostly all there. Amy and I have got the pods ready. I was just going to pick some wild flowers to put in there to make it look pretty. Then I need to get some baking done, so we have some snacks to offer. Greg has cooked some meals and frozen them, so if things get crazy, we have plenty of food to fall back on."

Lisa nodded. "I can do the wild flowers if you want, and then help with the baking."

"Thanks," Violet said, quickly eating the rest of the banana.

"Plenty of wood chopped?" Joseph asked.

"Yeah, Julie and Aragonite sorted that out," Greg said. "The main thing I need to do this morning before everyone starts arriving is rake the leaves from the parking area and the driveway, so no one slips on them."

"Perfect, I'll give you a hand with that," Joseph volunteered.

"Thanks."

Violet took the batter from Greg and heated up the griddle, while he made the tea. She heard the front door open and close. "We're all in the kitchen!" she called out.

Julie popped her head into the kitchen a few moments later. "Morning everyone! Mmm, that smells good."

"Morning, Julie," Greg said. "Coffee?"

"Yes please, Aragonite will have one too. He's just sorting the kids out, then he'll be over. How is everyone?"

Lisa sighed. "Good. A little tired. Joseph was having nightmares again last night."

Violet and Greg looked at one another. "What happened in them?" Violet asked, as she poured the batter onto the griddle in small amounts.

"I was in Atlantis and it was chaos. Word of your vision had got out, and everyone was panicking."

Violet sighed. "I had a dream this morning of when I had the vision."

"What do you think it means?" Julie asked. "Why is everyone suddenly remembering what happened in Atlantis?"

Violet flipped the pancakes and shook her head. "I don't know, but I do hope that we get some answers this weekend."

"Me too," Joseph agreed. "The lack of sleep is driving us both mad."

Lisa sipped her tea and nodded in agreement. "I nearly chucked him out the bed last night, just so I could get a few hours' proper sleep."

"Well, how about we set the intention right now that this weekend will bring us all the answers we need to be able to put these memories, these dreams, to rest?" Violet suggested.

Everyone nodded.

"Are you sure that you want to know?" Aragonite asked suddenly, appearing in the doorway. He accepted the mug of coffee offered to him by Greg.

Violet placed the first plate of pancakes on the breakfast bar and frowned at him. "What do you mean? Why wouldn't we want to know what happened? It's not like it will affect us now?"

Aragonite sipped his coffee and said nothing. Violet could see Julie looking at him strangely.

"Let's just intend for this weekend to bring us all what we need, whatever that may be," Greg said. "And leave it up to the Universe. It will be good to meet new and old friends, regardless."

Violet smiled at him and nodded, though the feeling of loss and devastation from her recent dreams and visions washed over her, and she wondered if Aragonite was right.

Did they really want to know what had happened? All those lifetimes ago?

She carried on making the pancakes, and asked the Angels for the strength to know the truth.

* * *

"What are you doing?" Gold asked.

Sarah looked up from the suitcase. "Packing," she replied with a smile. "I woke up this morning with the clearest message in my head – we must go to the Twin Flame Retreat this weekend."

"For the Atlantean Retreat? But we haven't been invited, and we haven't booked a place. Surely it will be full?"

Sarah sighed. "I'm certain it will be, but I'm also certain

we must be there. I'm sure we can stay in Greg's campervan if there's no room for us to stay in one of the pods."

"No room at the inn, eh?" Gold said with a chuckle.

Sarah joined in with his laughter.

"What about the children?" he asked.

"It's Gareth's weekend, he'll be picking them up soon. We just have to be there. We have to go. I don't even know why, which is irritating, believe me, but we need to go."

"Okay, I believe you. I will pack a few things."

"Good, we will need to hit the road soon to arrive by late this afternoon. I don't want to miss any of it."

Gold frowned. "Did you visit the Angels last night? Is that why you feel this urgent need to be there?"

Sarah shook her head. "I honestly don't remember any of my night-time journeys, I just woke with this overwhelming need to be there. That's it. No conscious information, just a feeling."

Gold nodded. "That's good enough for me. Shall I make us some sandwiches for the trip?"

"Yes that would be good. No pickle this time though, I hate it."

Gold smiled. "Yes ma'am. No pickle." He came over to her and kissed her. "Would you like some coffee too?"

"Yes please."

Gold left the bedroom, and Sarah sighed. She really wished she knew why she felt so strongly about travelling across the country to turn up unannounced at the Retreat. But she had long since stopped questioning her gut feelings, having accepted that they usually knew more than she did, and that she should just trust in them.

She closed the suitcase and zipped it up.

Whatever was to come, she would deal with it. She just hoped it wouldn't threaten her current happy existence with her Flame.

* * *

"Xander? What is it?"

Xander looked up from the cards in front of him, a frown etched deeply on his face. "I'm not sure, the cards and the Angels seem to be saying that something big is about to happen, but I can't figure out what."

Astrid moved to Xander's side, where he sat, cross legged in his meditation space.

"Big for us? Or for the world?" she asked, looking at the cards, but not really sure what she was looking for.

"Big for the world. A shift. A huge, cosmic shift. There's been a few recently, like the Flames reuniting against the odds, but this is bigger."

"You mean like me and you, and Louise and Oscar, and Delia and Quentin?" Astrid asked, mentioning her friends who had all recently reignited their connection with their Twin Flames.

"Yes. There have been more, too. People who have been for readings are getting together with Flames they thought there was no hope of reuniting with."

"Are the Angels giving any indication as to what the shift is? Or how it will happen?"

Xander looked off to his left side, then after a few moments sighed heavily. "No. They just want us to be prepared. But it's a bit difficult to prepare for something when you don't know what it is!"

Astrid touched his arm. "Perhaps they will share with us soon. Why don't you come and eat? Dinner is ready."

Xander smiled at her and nodded. "Yes, of course. I'm sorry, I didn't mean to make you wait. It smells great."

They went to the small dining area, and Astrid served the food. They had moved into the flat above the café, and despite being a little bit cramped with all their belongings in a small space, Astrid was really loving it. It felt much more like home than her previous flat. It was a much quicker commute to work too. She had taken over what Kirsty used to do, the accounts and stock ordering, and the rota and wages as well. It had been a steep learning curve, but she was enjoying it.

Although, if she was honest, she would probably enjoy just about any job if it meant that she got to spend every day with her Flame.

She sat opposite him and smiled as he began to tuck in. Even when stressed, he never lost his appetite. Especially for her cooking, which he seemed to think was amazing. She didn't tell him that she had been watching YouTube videos on how to cook his favourite meals, and that she wasn't a natural chef.

"I bumped into Walter today on my way back from the bank," she said, trying to think of conversation topics that didn't include prophesies of doom.

"Oh yeah? How is he?"

"He's good, he's having a Halloween party and has invited us. It's fancy dress. What do you think we should go as?"

As they debated the possibilities of costumes, Astrid was glad to feel the energy lighten around them, along with the mood. She put out a silent prayer to the Angels, that whatever the shift was, it wouldn't take her Flame away from her.

CHAPTER THIRTEEN

"I think it's time we got some help."

Ceri looked up at Charlie, and his heart hurt at the sight of the listlessness in her expression.

"Help?"

"I feel like you're slipping away from me, from us. And it's scaring the shit out of me right now."

Ceri looked back down at her hands. "Oh."

Charlie sighed. He didn't know what to do. He'd taken more time off work because after two weeks Ceri still wasn't able to do anything but sit on the sofa and watch TV. But he was running out of leave and was worried that it might put his job in jeopardy, which wouldn't make anything easier. He had hoped that the funeral would help to bring some closure, but Ceri had remained vacant.

"Please, baby," Charlie whispered, kneeling in front of her, taking her hands in his. "Tell me what I can do. What about the counsellor the hospital suggested? Or a support group?"

Ceri's gaze lifted a fraction to meet his. She shook her

head. "There's nothing you can do. He's gone."

Charlie closed his eyes for a moment and tried to breathe deeply. He opened them again. "I know he is, and I wish he weren't. But Juliet and I are still here. We are still here and we love you. We need you. We will never forget William, but he wouldn't want us to stop living because he isn't here."

Ceri frowned. "How do you know what he would want? He never got the chance to breathe, let alone speak."

Charlie could feel his patience slipping and he was desperately trying to keep his grasp on it. He did not want to lose his temper with his incredibly fragile, wounded wife. But he was afraid she might slip into a deep, dark hole of grief and never resurface.

"Ceri. I love you. I'm here for you, but I think you need to speak to someone. You can't carry this all inside you. It's not good for you, or for Juliet." Charlie waited for her to respond, holding her hands, and praying that his words would reach her in the depths of darkness where she was hiding.

He searched her eyes and thought he saw a tiny spark flicker in the blue. She sighed softly.

"There is a group, they meet up near here. I have the information, I just... wasn't ready to go."

"When do they meet?" Charlie asked carefully, not wanting to extinguish the flicker.

"Tuesday mornings."

Charlie squeezed her hands. "Can I take you there tomorrow morning?" After waiting what felt like an eternity, Ceri nodded, and Charlie felt relief flood through his body.

"I love you," he said, sitting on the sofa next to her, gathering her up in his arms. "We will get through this together, I promise."

A colourful flash out of the corner of his eye made him look up, and he saw his young daughter run into the room. She paused when she saw them on the sofa, and he held his hand out and waved for her to join them. She ran over to him and he pulled her close to him. He kissed her on the forehead and she looked up at him, and smiled.

"Dada!"

* * *

"Oh my goodness, could this place be any more magical?"

Both Vivi and Saphron stared out their windows at the bright red, gold and yellows of the trees they passed underneath, as they drove down the bumpy lane to the Twin Flame Retreat. They had been in the UK less than twenty-four hours but Saphron was already in love with the people and the architecture, as well as the rolling countryside they had just driven through.

"Is it really down here?" Henry asked, as they turned another corner, going deeper into the woods.

Sam, who was driving, shrugged. "No idea, you're the navigator!"

"Are we lost?" Vivi asked. "Will we end up in the Faerie Realm?"

"I saw a sign not far back, but we haven't seen a house yet, so it must be down here," Saphron said, not taking her eyes off the trees either side of them.

A few moments later, they saw a large wooden sign bearing the symbol of the Twin Flame Retreat.

"We're here!" Vivi exclaimed, bouncing up and down

in her seat.

Sam pulled the rental car into the last free space, and then turned off the engine. He twisted a little in his seat and smiled at the others. "We've made it. Looks like there's plenty of others here too. Let's go in, they're probably waiting for us. We are a bit later than we said we would be."

The light had already faded, but there were candles in jars lining their path as they walked up the driveway towards the house. There were fairy lights in the trees, and Saphron and Vivi couldn't stop themselves from exclaiming how beautiful it was. Even Henry chimed in with his agreement.

"It's just magical," Vivi breathed again as they reached the heavy wooden front door.

Before they could ring the bell, the door swung open, and a tall man with long dreadlocks stepped out towards them.

"Oh!" he said, when he saw them standing there in the porchlight. "I'm sorry! I didn't realise you were there. I was just popping out to get the firewood in. I'm Aragonite, you must be Saphron, Vivi, Henry and Sam, right?"

The group all nodded, and Aragonite ushered them into the front room, where the table was set for dinner.

"We're really sorry we're much later than planned," Sam said. "It took us an age to get out of London."

"It's all good, you're the last to arrive. The others are all in the lounge, it's a bit of a squeeze, so just find whatever space you can! I'm sure Violet will get the kettle on."

As if on cue, Violet poked her head around the doorway, her face lighting up when she saw Saphron and Vivi.

"Oh my goddess! You're here!" she exclaimed, rushing forward to embrace her friends.

Saphron giggled, then pulled back a little and looked at Sam and Henry. "Violet, this is Sam, and Henry. Guys, this is Violet."

Sam held his hand out to shake hers, but Saphron laughed as Violet threw her arms around each of them in turn, and kissed them on their cheeks. "It's so amazing to meet you two, finally. I've heard so much about you."

Sam raised an eyebrow and looked at Saphron who smiled. "Don't worry honey, it's all good stuff."

"Come on through, you have to meet everyone," Violet said, leading the way into the lounge. Saphron followed her Flame through, and when she saw everyone, she was amazed to realise she recognised their faces. She breathed in deeply, and knew that she was home here.

* * *

"Aragonite's been gone a long time," Julie commented to Violet in the kitchen, as they started to serve the meal for everyone. "He only went to get firewood."

Violet frowned as she put carrots on the plate Julie handed her. "Yeah, he has been gone a while. Do you want to go check he's okay?"

Julie nodded and Lisa took over her place to help with serving up. Instead of going through the overcrowded lounge, Julie ducked through the small wood hatch, where Aragonite should have been passing logs through.

She pushed the hatch closed behind her, and shivered. It had been a sunny day, but the temperature had dropped considerably. Autumn was well and truly here. She walked around the outside of the house, heading for the wood store. Her eyes adjusted to the moonlit path, and as she neared the wood store, she could hear voices.

She squinted into the darkness, wishing she had brought her phone with her for the torch.

"Aragonite?" she called out. Who would be visiting now? All the participants for the retreat had already arrived.

"I'm here," he called back. Julie followed his voice down the driveway, and saw him next to two figures. "We've got some surprise guests."

Julie tried to make out who they were, but in the gloom, couldn't make out their features. She reached Aragonite's side, still having no idea who they were.

"It's Starlight and Gold, Julie."

Julie eyes widened and her mouth dropped open. "Oh, wow, hello!" She held out her hand and Gold shook it. She could tell, even in the darkness that he felt uncomfortable. She and Sarah hugged.

"Did anyone know you were coming?" Julie asked. "Violet didn't mention it."

"No, it was kind of a last minute thing. I had this strong nudge to come here this weekend."

Julie nodded. "Well, we're a pretty full house, with everyone staying over, but I'm sure we can figure something out for you guys." She shivered again. "Come on inside, it's freezing out here."

She motioned for them to follow her, and Aragonite went to get the firewood in. As she walked back to the house, with two of the most powerful souls trailing behind her, instead of feeling excited, Julie felt an overwhelming feeling of dread, at the possible outcome of the weekend to come.

* * *

"Everyone is served, but we have some extras guests," Lisa announced, walking back into the kitchen. "Look who Julie found outside."

Violet and Greg looked up and saw Sarah and Gold behind her.

"Starlight!" Violet exclaimed, rushing forward to greet her sister. "What are you doing here? Is everything okay? Where are the kids?"

Lisa went to the sink to wash her hands, and Greg stepped forward to shake Gold's hand. "You look like you need a drink. Wine?"

Gold nodded, and Greg got the bottle opener and a bottle of red from under the counter.

Lisa's head was spinning from all the people who were crammed into Greg and Violet's house. They'd never had so many people there at one time before. The weirdest part was that Lisa felt like she'd known them all forever, despite only having met some of them for the first time that day.

She served herself some food, then went to join everyone in the front room. Joseph had saved her a seat next to him, so she sat down, her leg brushing against his under the table, giving her the shivers.

He smiled at her and she smiled back. She knew he'd felt the connection too.

"I am just so blown away that we're all here, in one place again. Everyone here was in Atlantis, right?" Dylan said.

Everyone nodded except for Aragonite, Ruby and Amy. "I was in the Angelic Realm. I chose not to go," Aragonite.

He looked at Julie, who smiled.

Lisa tucked into her food, feeling famished from all the frantic activity of the day, getting everything ready. She heard voices behind her, and turned to see Violet, Greg, Sarah and Gold come into the room, and there was a bit of shuffling about to make room for the two extras, but they managed it.

"Everything okay?" Violet asked before starting to eat. Everyone nodded or said yes. The silence was punctuated by the clinking of glasses and cutlery.

"So has everyone here been having the crazy dreams about Atlantis?" Joseph asked between mouthfuls.

"Oh yeah," Henry said. "They've been driving me crazy, they started up when I had the flu a few weeks ago."

"I've had quite vivid dreams of Atlantis," Jack said quietly. "I've been doing sketches of them, as soon as I wake up to see if I can work out their significance."

"Did you bring the sketches?" Violet asked. "I would love to see them. Everyone, Jack is the visual artist on the movie. We've been working together for months, but it was only a short while ago that Jack told me he was at the Academy with me, and in Atlantis."

"Who were you?" Dylan asked.

"Suede," Jack replied. "Professor of Cause and Effect."

"Oh wow, I knew you looked familiar!" Amy exclaimed. "I remember you now, you were just as quiet then too."

Jack chuckled. "Yes, I think that's why I only get a passing mention in the book." He winked at Violet who blushed.

"I already apologised for that," she said, sipping her wine.

"I'm just kidding," Jack assured her.

"So do you all know why you've been dreaming of Atlantis? Or why you are all here now?" Sarah asked.

Lisa looked around the room, and almost everyone was shaking their heads. "Do you?" she asked the Angel of Destiny.

Sarah frowned a little and glanced at Gold. "No, but I know that it felt important for us to be here. I think something big is going to happen this weekend, and there's part of me that's... afraid."

Violet reached across the table to touch Sarah's hand. "Afraid? What do you mean?"

Sarah looked around the room at the men and women gathered there. "There is a lot of power in this room right now. A lot of energy. Can't you feel it?"

Violet nodded. "Yes, but why is that something to be afraid of?"

Sarah shook her head. "I don't know yet, but I do know that we need to be sure to have protective energies in place, just in case."

There was silence again as everyone resumed eating, before the murmur of multiple conversations rose up over each other.

"You okay?" Joseph asked Lisa.

She looked down to realise she'd forgotten to keep eating. She put her fork down. Her stomach felt unsettled, nervous. What was going to happen this weekend? Julie had voiced her concerns to her before, after something Aragonite had said. Everyone had been having nightmares of the end of Atlantis.

"I'm fine, just, nervous, that's all," she replied.

Joseph reached over to squeeze her knee. "It'll all be okay, you'll see."

She nodded, but was finding it difficult to believe his words.

CHAPTER FOURTEEN

"Are you okay? You were really quiet tonight."

Maggie looked up at Steve as she unpacked her pyjamas to get ready for bed. "I'm okay," she said, pulling off her clothes and folding them up neatly. "Just a bit overwhelmed I guess. You know what it's like for me when I'm around too many people, I get a lot of visions."

Steve nodded. "I was quite overwhelmed, even without visions. It feels so weird to be meeting people I feel like I have known forever."

Maggie smiled while she got dressed for bed. "That's because you have known them forever. This group that has come together here was the most brilliant group of healers, inventors and creators in Atlantis."

Steve frowned. "You remember this? Or you had a vision of it?"

"I had a vision. Tonight, as everyone sat round the tables, eating, I was taken back to Atlantis, and I could see all the men around the table, discussing their latest project. None of what they said made much sense to me, but you were all very excited about it."

"Amazing," Steve said. "I wonder if we will find out more once we get together for the workshops tomorrow."

"I imagine you will," Maggie said, getting into bed. Steve quickly changed his clothes and got in with her. The small double bed in the pod was cosy, and Maggie felt instantly relaxed.

"I must admit, I don't really understand it all myself, I mean, if you hadn't said that I was an Atlantean, and that I needed to be here this weekend, I don't think I would have known that. I wouldn't have thought to come. I have no memories of Atlantis at all."

"I have the feeling that will change this weekend." Maggie smiled at him and kissed him goodnight. "I just hope you're ready to find out what it all means."

"Sounds ominous," Steve teased.

Maggie laughed but it sounded hollow. "I'm sure it will be fine." She reached out to switch the light off. They snuggled under the covers and Maggie closed her eyes.

"I love you," Steve whispered.

"I love you too," Maggie whispered back. "Forever."

* * *

"Don't make me leave, my love," Greg begged. "Please don't send me away to the seas. Let me stay here, be with you until the end."

Violet shook her head. "No, they need you, you must go. They will need a strong leader, a Seer, a healer. Without you, they will not thrive."

Her voice was weak, and her body was trembling.

"But how will I thrive without you?" Greg asked, tears running down his cheeks. "I love you, I'll love you for eternity."

Violet smiled. "Our love will outlast eternity itself." She reached up to wipe away his tears, then she reached out her arms and he gathered her thin frame into an embrace. Violet touched his neck, and a shudder went through her body. With a gasp, she woke up in bed, and the salty air, sound of the waves, and the sand beneath her feet disappeared.

"Violet, are you okay?"

Violet blinked and looked up at Greg, who was watching her, concern plainly written on his face. "I just remembered dying, in Atlantis. I changed you into a Merperson, then I died." Tears rolled down her cheeks. "You were devastated. You didn't want to leave me. But it was already too late, I was slipping away."

Greg closed his eyes, and Violet could see that he was struggling with his own emotions. "I dream of that moment sometimes too," he admitted.

"I'm so sorry I made you leave." She reached up to touch his cheek. "But I couldn't bear the thought of the world without you."

Greg leaned down to kiss her, and she tasted the saltiness of her own tears.

"I know that everyone seems to be afraid of what this weekend might bring, but I am hopeful that it will have a positive outcome, that we will discover the reason for our dreams and nightmares, and the reason for us all coming together like this." Violet whispered. She didn't think Sarah and Gold would be able to hear them talking from the next room, but she didn't want to chance it.

"I hope you're right," Greg said. "Because I have to admit, I've been feeling uneasy too. It all feels like it's being orchestrated somehow. Like the Angels are nudging us all again."

Violet sighed and rubbed the sleep out of her eyes. "It's not impossible. They might be operating under orders from someone other than Sarah."

She reached out to pick up her phone, and squinted at the time. It was only 6.30am. She set her phone down again and smiled at Greg. "It's too early to get up, what do you say we, well, you know?"

Greg smiled back and kissed her again, then they closed their eyes and fell asleep.

* * *

"Aria?"

Linen woke up with a start from a nightmare, and was surprised to see the other side of the camp bed empty. It wasn't like Aria to get up early.

He pulled the covers back and got up, slipping on his flip flops and a t-shirt, and a pair of shorts. Despite the early hour, it was still very warm. He stepped out of the small room they were staying in, and walked down the gloomy corridor, then stepped out of the front door into the glow of the sunrise. He scanned the street, still strewn with debris from the hurricane that had left thousands of islanders homeless. They had been there for weeks helping to rebuild homes and clear land. But it seemed like a never-ending task.

Aria was nowhere to be seen. Feeling slightly anxious

now, Linen breathed deeply and closed his eyes, trying to think where his Flame might have wandered off to. His eyes popped open and he smiled.

Of course.

He started walking down the street to a shelter where several families were living. They had been there the day before, and one of the families had a cat who'd given birth to kittens not long after the hurricane hit. Aria had become besotted by them, he would bet anything that's where she'd gone.

He reached the shelter and stepped inside, blinking to adjust to the lack of light. He headed for the small office area where the kittens were being kept in a box.

He reached the doorway, and saw a familiar blonde head. He leaned against the doorway and cleared his throat.

Aria jumped and spun around to see him, a kitten in her hands.

"Oh, Lin!" she said loudly. "You scared me!" She turned to set the kitten down in the box with its mum and siblings, then turned back again. "I didn't think you'd be up yet, I couldn't sleep."

Linen sighed. "I had another nightmare."

Aria frowned. "Again? Same thing?"

"Yes, I think so, it's fading now, it's hard to remember."

Aria looked back at the kittens for a few moments, then came over to Linen. She looked up at him. "These kittens remind me that even in the worst of circumstances, there can be bits of light, happy times, and adorableness."

Linen smiled. "Adorableness?"

Aria nodded. "Yes. Because even the smallest of things can make the biggest differences. Even a tiny candle can light up a dark room."

"Is there a reason why you're quoting a greeting card to me?"

Aria giggled. "Actually, my friend Amethyst told me that. But anyway, yes, what I'm saying is, even if your dreams are right, and they come true, there will be good things too. It won't all be bad."

Linen sighed. "I do hope you're right. Though I don't remember there being any kittens in any of the scenarios that played out."

Aria reached up on tip toes to kiss him. "Let's just enjoy the ones that are here then." She grinned. "Can we keep one?"

Linen shook his head. "No, no, absolutely not."

Aria raised an eyebrow. She followed Linen from the room, but called back to the kittens, "I'll see you soon, little Storm."

Linen groaned, and tightened his hand around Aria's. It looked like they might be about to become parents.

* * *

After a sleepless night of tossing and turning, Julie was relieved to finally see the sunlight filter through their thin curtains, lighting up the cabin. It was unlike her to have trouble sleeping, but after meeting everyone the night before, and experiencing the energy of all the Atlanteans together again, Julie had been too wired to drift off. She turned to look at Aragonite, who didn't seem to be having the same trouble. He was snoring gently.

She smiled and slid out from under the covers, shivering in the cool air. She grabbed her favourite fleece hoodie and slipped it on over her pyjamas. She went to check on the kids, who were, of course, all sleeping soundly. She peered at the clock. It was 6.30am. Too early to make much noise or get anything done. Without thinking too hard, she slipped on her wellies, and slipped out the door, closing it gently behind her. The air was even colder outside, and she shivered again. She decided to go for a walk, to warm up, and to hopefully shake off this weird feeling that was clinging to her.

A few yards down the lane, she was surprised to see a familiar figure up ahead. "Maggie?" she called out softly, hoping to not startle the Seer too much.

Maggie turned to look, a smile lighting up her face. "Good morning, Blue," she said, using Julie's Old Soul name. "Isn't it beautiful out here?" She waited for Julie to catch her up, and they fell into step together.

"It is. I have to pinch myself to remind myself I really live here. I mean, at some point, the cabin may get too small and we will have to think about moving into something bigger, but right now, the kids love it, Aragonite and I couldn't be happier, so I hope we can stay living locally."

Maggie nodded. "As much as I love our home, every time I visit here, I wonder why we don't live in more natural surroundings. It's so calming."

"So calming that you couldn't sleep?" Julie asked. "Or are you naturally an early bird?"

"I woke a while ago from a dream, and found I was too restless to fall asleep again, so I thought I'd go for a walk rather than disturb Steve."

"Same, except for the dream. What did you dream about?" Julie knew about Maggie's visions, and wondered if her dreams were also prophetic. She listened to the birds singing and the leaves crunching under their feet while Maggie paused before answering.

"It was of Atlantis, I think. The visions of that time, memories I assume, have been escalating."

"Do you think we're going to find out something big this weekend?" Julie asked, afraid of the answer but in need of answers all the same.

"I think that something will come to light that we are not aware of currently," Maggie said, and her vague answer made Julie even more curious.

"Do you know what it is?" she asked, ducking under a low branch as they walked further down the track.

Maggie sighed. "Not exactly. But it has something to do with the men who have gathered this weekend, and the fall of Atlantis."

Julie's eyes widened. "How are they related?" she asked.

Maggie shrugged. "I guess we will find out."

"I guess we will."

CHAPTER FIFTEEN

Breakfast was just as manic as the dinner had been the previous evening, even though Lisa had gone to the kitchen early to prepare. Julie was already there with Maggie, and Sarah was sipping a coffee in the corner, looking tired.

"Right, let's do this," Lisa said. "Julie, you're on drinks, Maggie, can you take the hot food in?" Both women nodded, and Lisa got started on the ingredients for the cooked breakfasts. "Oh, Sarah, could you sit in the front room and direct people to the cereals and cold drinks?"

Sarah nodded and left the kitchen. In all honesty, Lisa just couldn't concentrate with the Angel of Destiny sat in the corner, watching her. Her stomach had been doing somersaults all morning, after a restless night. Joseph had woken up gasping again, and Lisa was fed up with it. Despite her nervous butterflies, she couldn't wait to finally figure out what the hell was going on.

After they had served several breakfasts to early risers already, Violet and Greg entered the kitchen, looking a little dishevelled.

"Oh wow, you guys are amazing. Sorry, we fell asleep again." Violet and Greg looked at each other sheepishly and Lisa rolled her eyes and grinned. "Make yourself useful," she said, handing Greg two platefuls of veggie breakfast. "These are for Saphron and Vivi."

He nodded and took the plates into the front room. Violet went straight over to the kettle, and filled it up again, yawning widely.

"Bad night again?" Lisa asked, trying not to yawn herself.

Violet nodded. "Yeah, more dreams." She sighed. "Let's hope they stop after this weekend!"

"Amen to that," Lisa agreed. She flipped an egg and smiled at Violet. "Did you want a full brekki?"

Violet shook her head. "I think I'll go with cereal and toast this morning, thanks."

Lisa gave her full attention to the hot pans in front of her, and within half an hour, everyone had been served with their choice of food. She wiped her sweaty forehead with the back of her hand, and felt an arm wrap around her. She looked up to see Joseph. "Hey. Have you finished eating already?"

He nodded. "Have you eaten yet?"

"I'm just making myself a bacon buttie. Then I will sit down for a few minutes. Is Greg getting things ready for the first meditation?"

"I think so, he disappeared upstairs a little while ago. Shall I go check?"

"Please, he might need some help."

Joseph kissed her neck then left the kitchen. Lisa switched off the gas burners and placed the bacon into her awaiting roll. She put it on a plate, applied a generous amount of ketchup, then sat down at the breakfast bar. She felt too sweaty and smelly to join everyone in the front room. And she also felt the need for a little solitude too, before joining the women in the meditation tent.

The quiet lasted about two minutes before Violet, Julie and Maggie entered the kitchen, holding various dirty plates and cups. Lisa started to get up to help, but Violet waved at her to sit back down.

"We've got this," she insisted. "Sit and eat. You earned it. Everyone loved the breakfasts."

Lisa smiled and settled back down. She took a big bite of her roll, and savoured the taste. It wasn't often that she ate what she considered to be unhealthy food, but she felt she would need the sustenance to handle the day that was to come.

When she finished, she added her dish to the pile that Julie was washing up, and then went to have a quick shower, and get rid of the smell of grease.

As the water poured down her body, she closed her eyes and said a prayer to the Angels.

* * *

"Everyone comfortable?"

The group all nodded at Greg. The morning session was just going to be the men, and Greg was feeling quite nervous, and a little daunted by leading the meditation, knowing that he had some very powerful men in attendance, including Gold, who had asked to join in.

Greg could tell from her face at breakfast that Sarah had

wanted to be there too, but she hadn't spoken up.

"Okay, so close your eyes, and just to increase our awareness of each other, and our connection, I'm going to ask you to reach out either side of you and take the hands of those next to you."

He closed his eyes and reached out. He felt Joseph's hand clasp his left, and Sam's hand clasp his right. Their palms felt as sweaty as his, and he relaxed a little.

In a low voice, he led them through a maze before bringing them to a golden archway, which would lead them into Atlantis. He figured there was no point taking their time – they needed to get straight to the point and find out why they were there.

When they reached the archway, Greg took an involuntary deep breath, and stepped over the threshold. Suddenly, Joseph's and Sam's hands tightened around his, and he had the sensation of falling at speed through time.

When he came to a stop, he gasped for breath and looked around.

"It is time, Laguz," Sam said. "For the final piece."

Greg's eyes widened at his name, and then without thinking he replied. "I am ready. The design came to me in a vision last night. I know how it will be, Sowilo."

Sam smiled. "Then let us commence."

He followed Sam into a large room where a large machine sat, glimmering and shimmering as though it were made from crystals. It was both a surprise to Greg, and a familiar sight, as though he had been working on it for some time.

"I will need these things," he said, handing a piece of parchment to Sam. "Then I can finish it."

Sam took the paper and nodded. He disappeared into another room leaving Greg to stare at the machine, which he instinctively knew was their creation.

He blinked, and time appeared to have passed. When he looked around, the faces of the men in his home at the Retreat all looked back at him, all except Gold.

"It is finished," Jack said softly. "Shall we activate it?"

Greg nodded. "Yes, Kaunaz, please do the honours."

Jack nodded and moved towards the machine. He waved his hands over it in a complicated pattern, and it lit up, then began to hum. Instinctively, the men all formed a circle around it, and closed their eyes. Greg felt a rush of energy go through his body, making him feel like he was a young boy again. Every cell felt invigorated, made anew. He felt like he could run for miles.

He breathed in deeply, and opened his eyes, to find himself back in the Twin Flame Retreat.

"What was that?" Henry breathed, breaking the silence of awe.

"I felt so... young," Ben remarked. "When it was activated."

"I only got glimpses," Gold said. "What did you see?"

Greg let Jack explain what they had witnessed, as he tried to process it. It seemed as though they had invented something, something that made them feel young, and vibrant, and they had activated it. But what was it? And why was it linked to their nightmares? It had felt good, felt pure in intention.

Greg frowned, none of it made sense.

"I don't know about anyone else, but I have way too much energy to just sit here," Dylan remarked. "Can we take a break and come back in an hour? I need to go for a run or something."

Greg nodded. "Yes, take a break, and we will reconvene after lunch. I will ask Maggie if she wouldn't mind leading the next session, as I felt like I got too lost in it to be able to lead it effectively."

There were murmurs and nods of agreement, and Greg got up from his cushion, expecting to feel stiff from sitting still, but finding that he also felt quite energised and supple. It was as though the energy from the invention had come back with them through the meditation. Odd.

* * *

"I can't believe the morning disappeared so quickly!" Julie exclaimed as she helped Violet and Lisa serve up lunch.

"Time flies when you're having fun!" Vivi giggled. She took the plates from Violet, and put them on the dining table in the middle room.

Violet had decided that the women would have lunch separately to the men, so they could speak freely, and allow the men to discuss their morning session. Aragonite was joining the men, although he hadn't joined in their session. Julie was desperate to find out what had happened, but none of the men had seemed willing to divulge. She was hoping Aragonite might have more luck getting some information.

When she joined her sisters at the lunch table, she forgot her curiosity for a while, as they all discussed which lifetimes had been their favourite previous to this one.

"I don't think many of my lives could beat working at the Academy," she said. "I remember it being the most peaceful time of my existence, yet I felt I was fully living my purpose, fully myself."

"I agree," Saphron said. "We were really making a difference there, teaching the Earth Angel Trainees how to be human. I would go back there and do it all over again in a heartbeat."

"I miss it sometimes," Violet admitted. "Being on set the last few months, watching it being acted out by other people really made me appreciate what we had there. And yes," she said, looking at Saphron. "The difference that we were making to the world."

"You don't feel like we're making a difference here?" Maggie asked quietly. There was something weird about her tone, which Julie couldn't put her finger on.

Violet sighed. "I know we are, but well, don't you feel like sometimes it's just not quite enough? That the world is Awakening, but not fast enough? It feels like the world is still out of control, and that the improvements are slow to come, and I wonder if we actually ever will make it to the Golden Age."

The other women nodded in agreement. "It doesn't feel like enough," Vivi agreed, unusually serious for a moment. "It feels like we have taken too long to feel confident enough to stand up and be counted."

"Or we have been busy with the human necessities of raising children, making a living and keeping up appearances," Julie remarked, thinking over her life with her ex-husband.

"How could we have done it any differently though?" Saphron asked. "I do feel we did the best that we could, and that there's still time, we can still turn things around."

"I hope you're right," Violet said. "I can't wait for the movie to come out, only so that the Awakening will happen on a bigger scale."

"I can't wait to see it! Saphron said. "I hope they got someone gorgeous to play me!"

Everyone laughed and the conversation shifted to discussing the movie, and Julie tried to concentrate on her meal, and not try to eavesdrop on the conversation filtering through from the other room.

* * *

"When you step over the threshold into the light, you will be back in Atlantis, experiencing the last moment you remember. I will allow you to experience it for a while, and then will guide you back. If at any point, it becomes uncomfortable, please just come back, even if I have not called you."

Maggie took several deep breaths, and then with her hands firmly in Greg's and Sam's grip, she stepped over the threshold. She knew that the contact she had with them would allow her to enter their memories, so she could see what they saw.

She blinked in the bright light, and her eyes widened at the sight before her. A machine that defied description pulsed and glowed in front of her. She looked for any clues as to what it was, or did, but all she could feel was that it was altering her cells.

She looked around the room for Laguz, and found him scribbling in the corner, at a crystal table. She went over to him, and tried to read his writing, but it was illegible. It was symbols and dashes that she didn't recognise.

"Laguz, it is perfect already, why do you insist on trying to change it?"

Maggie looked up to see Jack, the quiet artist.

"I just want to be sure our calculations are correct."

"You know that they are. Ailments are already clearing, illnesses are disappearing, people are looking younger and healthier than ever, it is working!"

Greg looked up at Jack and nodded. "You are right. I will stop." He put away his notes, and rose up. "I do feel the effects of it, do you?"

Jack smiled. "I feel like a young man again." He gazed at the machine. "To live forever, what a beautiful concept."

Maggie gasped, glad she was but a shimmering glimpse within the reality she observed. They had invented a machine that would give them eternal life?

She followed Greg as he left the room, which was in fact a cave, and she kept close as he wove his way through the maze towards the entrance. She followed him home, and saw him greet Velvet, who was waiting for him at home, playing their song on the piano.

"My love," she said when she finished the piece. "I have been waiting for you, I have some news."

Greg frowned. "What is it? Are you well?"

Velvet grinned and took his hand, placing it on her stomach. "I am most certainly well."

Greg's eyes grew wide. "You are… you are pregnant?"

Velvet nodded and they kissed. "It's a miracle. She is our miracle."

"She?" Greg breathed. "How do you know?"

"I have seen her. In a vision. She came to visit me."

Violet kissed him again. "She has your eyes, and my smile."

Maggie watched them embrace again, her eyes prickling with tears. She knew that just a few months later, Velvet would lose the child, and Atlantis would be no more. But where did it all go wrong?

She pulled back, and tightened her grip on Sam's hand, to see if she could enter his memory, but it was all beginning to fade away.

"Slowly leave where you are, and follow my voice back to the tunnel, back to the Retreat," she said softly out loud, hoping not to startle anyone. After a few moments, she spoke again. "When you are ready, open your eyes and come back to the room."

She opened her eyes, and found herself gazing into Greg's. Tears were flowing freely down his cheeks. "She would have had green eyes, and Violet's smile."

Maggie nodded, and squeezed his hand before releasing it.

Everyone shared the individual memories they had experienced, and Greg shared that the invention was meant to have given them eternal life on Atlantis. There were looks of remembrance and recognition on some of the men's faces, as they understood the enormity of the power they had created.

"But what went wrong?" Steve asked. "How was Atlantis destroyed?"

Maggie had a sneaking suspicion, as her vision of the circle of men came to mind, but she would wait to see what else was uncovered before speaking up.

CHAPTER SIXTEEN

Astrid approached the door to Xander's reading room, her heart pounding, and fear coursing through her. She could feel that something was really wrong, and judging by the looks on the faces of everyone who had left there that morning, she was right. She knocked softly, then entered without waiting to be called in.

She blinked in the gloom, her eyes adjusting slowly. She saw Xander sitting at the table, his head in his hands.

She rushed over to his side, and knelt by his chair. "Xander, what is it? Please, tell me, I'm scared, I have this awful feeling and I cannot shake it."

Xander looked at her, and his eyes gave her chills. "It's all over," he whispered.

Astrid frowned. "What is? What are you talking about?"

Xander picked up his cards and dropped them onto the table. "Everything. Every reading I have done has foretold the end. I cannot hide it from those who have come here to find out their future. It is too clear from the cards. There is no future. For any of us."

Astrid's heart stuttered. "The end of everything? That is what the Angels are saying? The cards? Are you sure? What is going to happen?" When Xander didn't reply straight away, she gripped his arm. "Please, you're scaring me. What's going to happen?"

Xander shook his head. "I don't know, but it will be soon. The world is about to shift, and there's nothing we can do about it."

* * *

"Hey, what is it?"

Louise looked up from her phone at Oscar, tears streaming down her cheeks. "It's my mum, she's been taken ill."

Oscar pulled her into a hug. "Oh no, do we need to go there? I can drive you right now."

Louise breathed in his scent, and tried to hold back the sobs. "She's gone into surgery, my dad said he would call when she comes out."

"What's wrong? Did he say?" Oscar pulled back to look at her.

She shook her head. "They're not sure, she had really bad stomach pains, and they thought it might be an obstruction of some sort. It's been going on for days, but it only got really bad today." She sniffled. It was so typical of her dad to refuse to reach out until things were too bad.

"I'll take you there right now. What hospital?" Oscar was already moving towards the door to get his coat, and Louise realised this must be bringing things up for him, as he hadn't got to the hospital for James before he died. She stood up, her knees a little shaky.

"It's Worcester General," she said, grabbing some tissues to wipe her face. She grabbed her handbag and tucked her phone inside.

"We can be there in two hours, if traffic is with us."

Louise met Oscar at the door. He kissed her on the forehead and hugged her again. "Let's go."

She nodded and locked the door before they headed for his beaten up car.

The journey passed in a blur. Louise sent her dad a message to say they were on their way, but had received no response. She prayed as hard as she could that she would see her mother again, that she would come out from the op, and smile at her, and tell her that everything was going to be okay.

When they reached the hospital, darkness was quickly falling, and after parking and making their way through the maze of corridors, they arrived on the ward to find her father hunched over in the plastic chair.

"Dad," she whispered, choking up at the sight of his defeated body. He looked up, his eyes red, his forehead scrunched up.

"Oh, Lou," he said, rising up to hug her. "I'm so sorry I didn't message sooner, I really didn't think it was anything to worry about, and your mother said not to bother you."

"It's okay, I'm here now. And, well, this is Oscar."

The two men awkwardly shook hands, and her dad nodded. "Nice to meet you, I'm sorry it's not in better circumstances."

"I'm sorry too, have you had any news?"

With those words, Louise heard someone clearing their

throat softly behind her. They all turned to see the doctor standing there. She didn't even need to hear his words to know what he was going to say.

Her mother had gone home to the Angels.

* * *

"I can't believe you won't tell me what you found out yesterday in the mediations. In fact, none of the men, nor Maggie will say what happened." Violet frowned at Greg across the pillow. "Did you all sign a non-disclosure agreement or something?"

Greg chuckled. "No, I think we all just feel like we only have a few puzzle pieces right now, and we need more before we can work it all out. If feels like if we talked about it too much, we might scare it away."

Violet raised an eyebrow. "Hmm, I'm sure the memories aren't going anywhere. Although, I didn't dream of it last night, so maybe whatever you are doing is healing it?"

Greg shrugged. "Maybe." He leaned forward to kiss her. "You know, we need to get up soon, and we can either talk, or we can, do other things…"

Violet shook her head. "You always know how to distract me so I don't ask questions. But as much as I would love to, the girls and I have plans for a walk this morning, so you guys are on your own for breakfast."

Greg groaned. "But Lisa's breakfasts are way better than mine."

Violet pecked him on the lips then got up, and put her dressing gown on to go to the bathroom. "Tough."

She got ready quickly, deciding to have a shower when

she got back. They were going to walk down to the river, and she knew she would be sweaty when they got back. She went back to the bedroom to get dressed. Greg had fallen asleep again and was snoring gently.

She shook her head and smiled. She was still a little irked that he refused to share any details of the meditations, but she couldn't stay mad at him for more than five minutes, she loved him too much.

Once wrapped up warm, she left the bedroom, and made her way downstairs. Sarah was already drinking a cup of coffee in the kitchen.

"Morning," she said softly. "Did you sleep okay?" She hadn't had a proper chance to speak with Sarah alone, and she still had no idea why she had felt so compelled to come for the weekend.

"Not really. My dreams were chaotic, muddled. I couldn't figure out what was happening. It was exhausting, to be honest."

Violet frowned. "I didn't dream at all, I don't think. I was hoping that it meant that things were healing."

Sarah sighed. "I do hope things get sorted this weekend. So are we still heading to the river? I liked the sound of the ritual Lisa spoke of."

Violet nodded and glanced at the clock. "Yes, we'd better get shifting." She took a basket down that was hanging from the ceiling, and filled it with fruit, and some flapjacks and homemade cakes, and then filled two flasks, one with tea, and one with coffee.

"Right, shall we?"

Sarah nodded and finished her coffee, picking up her coat and following Violet to the door. Once outside, Violet breathed in the crisp air deeply. She loved the autumn. Despite the death and decay of the leaves from the trees, it was so incredibly beautiful.

She and Sarah made their way down the path to where the rest of the women were waiting. Violet smiled at them all. "Morning! Are we all ready?"

"I know I am! As soon as Lisa said about releasing our beliefs and our pasts, and our 'not good enoughs', I knew I wanted in!" Vivi said, hopping up and down a little on the spot.

"Amen to that," Julie chimed in. "Let's release the past!"

"Lead the way," Maggie said to Violet.

Violet nodded and the group set off down the path, deep into the woods, to the river, where they planned to release their old beliefs by bathing naked in the flowing water. Violet just hoped that there were no early morning dog walkers out on that Sunday morning.

* * *

"You didn't tell the others?"

Sarah looked up from the mirror where she was applying her makeup and shook her head. "No, Gold, I didn't tell the others. At this point in time, I don't really know what it all means, which frustrates me. Until we know for sure what's going on, I thought it best that I not say anything."

"Oh, good. Because the others have remained quiet, and I realised perhaps I shouldn't have told you."

Sarah smiled at him. "I'm sure they would forgive you." She concentrated on finishing her makeup, then went to her suitcase and dug out her warmest jumper. The river had been freezing, and despite getting dry, she still felt a bit chilled through. She pulled the jumper over her head, and looked at Gold again, who was watching her every move.

"What is it?"

Gold sighed. "I have this... feeling... that we are not long for this world."

Sarah frowned. "What do you mean?"

"When I first got here I struggled so much. Being human. It's hard, but now, I have come to love the smells, and sounds, and feelings that come with this heavy body. But now that I don't mind it, it feels like it's fading away."

Sarah crossed the room and wrapped her arms around him. "What's going to happen? Is it because of this weekend?"

"It would make sense. Why else would we be here?"

Sarah felt tears beginning to form. "I have become used to being human too. I don't wish to go home yet."

"I'm not sure any of us will have a choice. Someone will act soon, and change everything, much like Velvet did, all those years ago."

Sarah frowned. "The timelines," she breathed. "You think someone will change the timelines?"

"It's the only thing that will cause the massive shift that I can feel is coming."

Sarah gripped him tighter in her arms. "I love you."

"I love you too, Starlight. Whatever happens, promise me, you will find me."

"I promise."

CHAPTER SEVENTEEN

Charlie watched his daughter running around the park, kicking the piles of leaves and giggling, and his heart felt lighter than it had in a long time. Ceri was at home with two friends from the support group, and they were teaching her how to knit. The group knitted tiny hats and booties for an organisation that sent clothes out to parents of stillborn babies. Since getting some support, Ceri had begun to take part in life again. Charlie had gone back to work, and was no longer in danger of losing his job.

Things were getting better. He just wished that the nightmares that plagued him at night would go away.

"Dada! Dada!" Charlie snapped out of his thoughts and smiled at his daughter.

She twirled about, and then lost her balance and fell over. Charlie paused before jumping up to rush to her aid, and sure enough, she giggled and jumped up, then carried on running around. The park was quiet for a Sunday morning, and Charlie was thankful. He wasn't in the mood for the chatter of other parents trying to draw him into conversation.

He was trying to figure out why he kept dreaming about Atlantis.

At least, he thought it was Atlantis. Aside from the weird vision he'd had of a life he'd lived alone, until the world had ended abruptly, he'd not had any visions or dreams of other lives. Until now. He had been writing down the snippets he could remember from his dreams, and was trying to piece them together, but aside from having recognised Violet there, and knowing that they were not together at that time, he hadn't been able to work any more of it out.

Before the dreams had started, he hadn't thought about Violet in a long time. Despite having been so obsessed with her, so in love with her, his feelings had dissipated when Ceri had entered his life. And he finally understood the power of the Twin Flame connection. He had no idea where Violet was, although he had read her book. But he hoped she had also found her Flame, and that she was happy.

Maybe one day he would get to thank her for Awakening him.

* * *

"Everyone ready?"

The men all nodded, by now used to the routine, and they all, in unison, reached out to hold each other's hands, and Greg felt the energy rush around the circle. He closed his eyes and led them through the maze. He had hoped Maggie would lead again, but she insisted she needed to rest.

When they reached the Golden archway to Atlantis,

Greg felt his body shudder as he stepped into the past.

"What should we call her?"

He smiled at Violet. "I think we should call her Rose," he replied. They were walking through the village, hand in hand. He glanced down at her, and his heart swelled with love and pride. He wished he could tell her why it was suddenly possible for them to have a child, but he and the others had sworn each other to secrecy. They would not speak of their invention to anyone.

"Rose. I like that. She will be as beautiful as a rose. It will fit perfectly."

Greg smiled at his Flame, and squeezed her hand. Suddenly the world shifted and he was in bed, having awoken to find Violet gone. He found her by the window, staring out at into the darkness. He wrapped his arms around her.

"What is it?" he whispered to her.

She was silent for a while, and all Greg could hear were the waves crashing on the rocks. "I had a dream."

"Was it a bad one?" Both of them being Seers, prophetic dreams were fairly typical, but he hadn't seen her so upset about one before.

She nodded, and more tears flowed down her cheeks. He tightened his grip. "Tell me about it." He waited patiently until she managed to utter the words.

"I had a vision, yesterday, of the end of our world," she whispered. Greg stiffened and his heart started to thump loudly.

"So I prayed before sleep to be given a solution to save our people."

Greg swallowed. "Did you dream of a solution?"

Violet nodded, her jaw tight. "Yes. I did."

Greg sighed in relief. "So there is a way to avoid this fate?"

"For most, yes."

Greg frowned and stood straight, turning Violet around so he could look her in the eye. Her tear-stained face was lit only by the candlelight that spilled out from their bedroom. "What do you mean, for most?"

Violet met his gaze, her expression pained. "For you. You will be saved."

"But not you?" Greg's heart stopped.

Violet shook her head. "Nor our child." She rested her hand on the barely visible bump under her nightgown.

Greg felt tears running down his face, soaking his shirt. "How long?"

The world shifted again, leaving Greg breathless in the transition. It was a scene he knew well, that had haunted his dreams for many years.

It was their final goodbye.

Unable to bear the crushing sorrow of leaving her lifeless body there on the beach, Greg forced himself out of the vision, and spoke out loud, to guide the other men back too.

He released Dylan's and Jack's hands, and took a cloth handkerchief from his pocket, to blow his nose and wipe his eyes. He saw the others looking equally as shocked and in pain.

"Did anyone get any new information? I saw myself leaving for the seas, but I didn't see how it ended."

"I did."

Everyone turned to look at Jack, his quiet voice laced

with shame and sorrow. "I know how it ended." He looked at each man in turn.

"And it was all our fault."

* * *

"Maggie? Are you okay? Maggie!"

Violet rushed over to where her friend had just collapsed onto the floor, and knelt by her side. She turned her over, and it appeared as though she were having a fit of some kind.

"Put her into the recovery position," Julie said, joining Violet on the floor. They both moved her into a safe position, and Violet brushed Maggie's hair from her face.

"Get Steve, quickly," Violet said to Lisa.

Lisa jumped up and ran upstairs.

"Is she breathing?" Saphron asked. "Shall I call an ambulance?"

With that, Maggie gasped and her eyes flew open. She looked up at their concerned faces, her eyes wide.

"Oh, Maggie," Violet said, relief flooding through her. "You scared the crap out of me. Are you okay?" She helped her up and sat her on the sofa. Lisa returned with Steve, who rushed to his Flame's side.

"What happened?"

"I need some water," Maggie said.

"I'll get it." Violet went to the kitchen, her hands shaking slightly as she filled the glass from the tap. For a moment, she thought her friend had left the Earth, and the idea of it had shaken her. Could the weekend get any stranger?

She returned to the lounge with the glass of water, which

Maggie drank quickly, then handed back the empty glass.

"Thank you. I'm okay, I think it was just a vision, but the details... they're hazy now." She looked at Steve. "Did something just happen upstairs?"

Steve's eyes widened. "Actually, yeah, we were just about to find out what happened in Atlantis, why it was destroyed."

"You were?" Violet asked. She looked around at her sisters. "Do you know what? I think this separation has gone on long enough. This is something we all need to hear, as it is affecting all of us."

She gestured to Maggie, who was beginning to regain some colour in her cheeks. The women all nodded.

"I'll go and let them know," Julie said, heading for the workshop room.

"I don't know if that's a good idea," Steve started.

"I don't care. This has been the oddest weekend ever, we are all having nightmares and it's time to find out what the hell is going on," Violet said, leaving no room for discussion. She grabbed some cushions from the sofa, and Saphron and Vivi followed suit.

Within five minutes, everyone who was on site that weekend was crammed into the workshop room, in a vague circle. Greg had tried to protest, but Violet was adamant.

Once everyone was settled, they all turned to look at Greg, who looked very uncomfortable.

"Right, well, um, so we just did another meditation, and during it, Jack saw something that will explain what happened, so um, Jack, over to you."

Jack looked even more uncomfortable than Greg with everyone's attention on him, and Violet's heart was thumping painfully.

"So, first of all, in Atlantis, we created something. A machine that healed cells that would essentially have prolonged our lives, forever."

Violet's eyes widened and she glanced at Greg. They invented a machine to make them live forever?

"And it worked. Ailments were clearing up, people felt young again, disease was eradicated, and everything was good," Jack continued.

"But?" Sarah asked impatiently.

"But it only lasted for a few months, and then, for no reason, the machine began to... malfunction."

"I don't remember that?" Sam said. "Wouldn't we have known?"

Jack shook his head. "No one but me kept an eye on the machine. Everyone was too busy living their lives, feeling healthier and younger than they'd ever felt. We had built the machine to last for an eternity, and no one imagined it would ever break down. But for some reason, it did. I tried to fix it, but it was beyond me."

"Why didn't you say something? Why didn't you ask for help?" Greg asked.

"By the time I was about to, word of Velvet's premonition has spread, and I knew it would be too late. I didn't want anyone else to bear the burden of the fact that we had created the very thing that was to destroy us."

"Wait a minute," Violet said. "Are you saying that it was your machine that destroyed Atlantis?"

"Yes, I was there when it imploded, as was Joseph, and Ben. They had guessed what was going on, and also chose to stay behind."

There was a shocked silence in the room.

"I can't believe it. Are you sure? It was our fault?" Dylan asked.

Jack sighed. "It's true. It was all our fault."

Violet felt sick. Her memories of Atlantis swirled around her, and she realised that she had lost everything – her home, her child, her love and her life – all because of the selfishness of the men in that room. Including her own Flame.

She stood up abruptly. "Excuse me." She stumbled out of the room, ignoring her friends calling her name. She was filled with rage and knew she needed to get as far away from everyone as possible. She went downstairs, grabbing her coat and her boots on the way. She shoved her feet into her boots and walked quickly down the driveway.

She had never felt so betrayed. And in that moment, she hated Greg more than she had ever hated anyone in her life.

* * *

"She's my friend too, I'm fine, let me go and look for her."

Maggie looked at Steve, who had been refusing to allow her to join everyone who was searching for Violet. It had been four hours since she had walked out of the house, and Greg was out of his mind with worry. Maggie could sense her friend's despair, and she had an idea of where Violet would be, but felt she needed to be the one to find her.

"I will be fine, I'll take my phone, and I will send a message as soon as I find her, okay?"

"Do you know where she is? Tell me, and I'll go."

Maggie sighed. "Steve, please trust me. She's just had

the biggest shock of her existence, and I don't think she will want to see you, or anyone else who played a part in it right now."

Steve hung his head and Maggie felt bad. But she knew that she needed to leave.

"I will message the moment I find her." She reached up to kiss him, then went past him to the door of the pod. She set off down the path, and could hear the others calling Violet's name in the distance. She had only been to the caves once before, but she was certain that it was where Violet was. Because it was the one place that she had been forbidden to go to, since the cave-in and Hannah's accident several years before.

Maggie got to the fence covered in danger signs, and climbed over. She went carefully down the bank, but still skidded and slipped on the fallen leaves. She breathed a little easier once she had gone through the tunnel, and was in the clearing. She approached the mouth of the largest cave, and sure enough could see Violet's familiar red coat. She moved out of sight and got her phone out. She sent a message to Steve, and then put it back into her pocket, and approached her friend slowly.

"I should have known you'd find me," Violet said. She smiled but there was no warmth or humour in it.

"I'm sorry it took so long. Steve wouldn't let me go at first." Maggie reached the mouth of the cave, and then carefully sat on a mossy rock, a couple of feet away from where Violet sat. "Everyone is really worried. Greg is going out of his mind."

"Good."

Maggie winced at her tone. "He loves you, Violet. No

matter what happened in Atlantis, or whose fault it was, he loves you."

"He destroyed it all. Our home, our child, our city, my life and now my love for him."

"You don't mean that," Maggie said softly. "He's your Flame, you love him more than anything."

"I did," Violet said, looking Maggie in the eye. "But the moment I realised that he was the reason why I lost my child, and our life together, something snapped. Something died inside me all over again. I hate him so much right now. I can't even bear the thought of seeing him, or any of the others. I hate all of them."

Maggie heart thudded as she heard the truth in Violet's words. Suddenly, she could see Violet alone in a dark room, staring out of a window, grief and pain etched into her older features. Maggie knew then that the possibility of the future she had seen, with Violet on the stage and the Rainbows about to arrive, had gone.

"We could have grown old together, and watched our child grow up," Violet said softly, bringing Maggie back to the present.

"What if the only reason you were pregnant was because of the machine?" she asked suddenly, remembering the meditation.

Violet frowned. "What do you mean?"

"You had tried for years to get pregnant, but it never happened. But you got pregnant within weeks of the machine being activated. I saw it. I saw you tell Laguz you were pregnant. He knew it was because of the machine."

Violet was quiet for a while. "Why would he create a machine to give us a child, only to have it destroy us months later? Why bring that joy and hope only to kill it?" A sob escaped from her. "It makes no sense, Maggie."

Maggie got up and moved closer to Violet, wrapping her arms around her friend, who was now crying and shivering.

"I don't understand either. But I do know that the intentions of those men were pure. They had created a machine to give us all eternal life, so that we could live in our own heaven on Earth. Death and destruction was not in their hearts or minds. So whatever went wrong was just a terrible mistake. But I don't think they should be punished for eternity for it."

"How can I ever forgive him though? Right now the thought of him just makes me feel sick."

"We will find a way through," Maggie said softly, even though she had a feeling that it wouldn't be possible.

The damage had been done.

CHAPTER EIGHTEEN

"I'm so worried. It's dark now, are you sure Maggie found her? Are you sure she's safe?"

Sam wrapped his arms around Saphron, and Steve answered her questions from across the room.

"Yes, Maggie sent me a text. I assume that they're just talking, but if they're any longer, I will call her and see where they are."

Everyone was huddled into the lounge, trying to warm up after scouring the woods all afternoon for Violet. Saphron watched Greg pacing back and forth in the kitchen. She had tried to comfort him, but he was unresponsive.

"So what are we going to do about this?" Henry asked. "We've just discovered that the men in this room were responsible for the fall of Atlantis, and shaped the rest of human history for all time. There must be a reason for us gaining this knowledge now."

"Like what? I just feel horribly guilty," Dylan said. "What am I going to say to Ruby when I get home? Hi, honey, I destroyed the world?"

"I don't think guilt was the purpose of this discovery," Ben said thoughtfully. "Did you feel the energy? From the machine?"

The men all nodded. "Do you still feel it now?" Ben asked. "I've had a really bad back for months, but after the meditation where we activated the machine, the pain vanished, I mean, completely gone. Like I never had a bad back at all."

"My shoulders feel a lot better," Jack said quietly.

"And my stomach has never felt more settled," Sam said. "But what are you trying to suggest?" he asked Ben.

"If it was possible to feel the benefits of the machine and bring those benefits into this present moment, shouldn't it be possible to take this knowledge into the past and affect the outcome?"

"Wait a minute," Sarah said. "Are you suggesting what I think you're suggesting?"

"I'm suggesting we change it. We go back to Atlantis, and we fix the glitch."

There was silence as everyone absorbed the meaning of his words, then the room erupted into a cacophony of voices.

But Sarah's was the loudest.

"Absolutely not. I cannot allow it. Do you have any idea what you would be doing?"

Everyone stopped talking and looked at the Angel of Destiny.

"If the machine indeed worked okay, and had continued to work, that would mean you would all still be there, right now. You would have lived forever, in those lives, in those bodies. The Merpeople wouldn't have been created, the world as we know it now would cease to exist." She looked at Aragonite. "You would still be in the Angelic Realm, I would still be in the stars with Gold. There would be no Earth Angels, no Twin Flame Retreat."

"Where do I sign up?"

Everyone turned to see Violet standing in the doorway with Maggie, and Saphron sighed in relief. She saw Greg rush from the kitchen and hug his Flame, but Saphron could see he got no response from her.

"But it's possible? It could work?" Sam asked. "We could go back in time and change it, so that Atlantis was never destroyed, and we all lived for eternity?"

Saphron looked at Sarah, who was shifting about uncomfortably. "It's a possibility. I don't know if it would work. There is a lot of powerful energy in this group, and if you were able to bring back the benefits of the machine, then yes, there is a possibility that you could go back and change things. But it's too big. It will create untold ripples. Do you all really want to be responsible for the deaths of most of the people on this planet?"

"The world's going to hell in a handbasket anyway, so what does it matter?" Violet asked. She walked through the lounge to the kitchen, and Saphron got up to follow her.

"Violet?" she said softly.

Violet looked up. Her cheeks were red from the cold and her eyes were bloodshot. "I'm sorry. Disappearing like that was incredibly unprofessional of me. But the pain was too much."

Saphron nodded and wrapped her arms around her friend. "I understand. I was angry too. I couldn't believe that Sam had a part in this either. But maybe… maybe this is our second chance? Maybe this is our time with them now? Maybe we can finally grow old with our Flames?"

"I just don't know if I want to anymore. He's not the person I thought he was."

Saphron gripped her tighter. "Give it time, just let yourself heal before you decide."

* * *

"Please, Violet, please talk to me."

Greg's heart was thudding painfully in his chest, as he watched Violet undress and get ready for bed. He had the feeling that if they hadn't had so many people staying over, she would have slept in another room, just to be away from him.

"Just leave it," she said, refusing to look at him.

"I can't. I need to know what's going through your head. I'm devastated that what I designed destroyed Atlantis, but please, please know that I had no idea. I would never have stopped trying to fix it if I had known. I would never have left you there if I'd realised it was my fault."

"But you did leave me there," Violet spat. "I lost my baby, I lost you, and then I lost my life. All because of you. I saved you! I couldn't bear the thought of the world without you, but you were the one who ruined it!"

Violet looked at him and Greg saw the tears streaming down her cheeks. "You carried on living, while I died, and lived the next several hundred lifetimes without you. It's no wonder I blocked you out of my memory. Why would I want to remember the man who destroyed everything I loved? Maybe a Twin Flame relationship isn't the perfect union after all."

"Don't you think that's a bit harsh? I had no idea," Greg insisted. "Until Jack told us, just a few hours ago, I had no idea that the machine had malfunctioned. And I didn't even remember the machine existed until yesterday!" Greg sighed, and tried to lower his voice. "I love you, Violet. And it is tearing me apart knowing that it was my fault that we lost Rose."

Violet frowned. "That's the name of the daughter I was told I would have with someone else."

"I know, but it is also the name I suggested we call our child in Atlantis. The memory appeared in the meditation yesterday. You told me she would have my eyes, and your smile. You had seen her in a vision."

More tears cascaded down Violet's cheeks, and Greg wondered if he shouldn't have shared that. He went around to her side of the bed, and without giving her a chance to reject him, he wrapped his arms around her and held her tightly.

"I would never, ever, have knowingly harmed you. I designed the machine because I wanted to be with you forever. Because I never wanted to ever have to let you go. And yet, because of my selfish desire, I lost you anyway, over and over. I didn't just carry on my life as normal when I became a Merman, I mourned you every single day. And I wished with everything I had that I'd perished with you in Atlantis."

Greg could feel her shoulders shaking, and he rested his cheek on her head. "I love you, Violet. I am so, so sorry for what happened."

Violet pulled away, and Greg loosened his grip a little. "I know. But I don't think I'm quite ready to forgive you yet." She closed her eyes. "Or if I ever really will."

* * *

"What are we doing today?" Aragonite asked Julie. He had missed the drama of the previous day, as he had been taking care of the kids.

Julie sighed. "I think they're going to do one more meditation to try and heal any guilt or shame or bad feeling surrounding what happened in Atlantis. Then everyone will leave in the afternoon." She looked at her Flame. "It really was a bit of a crazy weekend. No wonder you had bad feelings about it."

Aragonite sighed. "It did feel like it would be a bit of a shitshow."

Julie laughed, not expecting those words to come from the former Angel. "Shitshow?"

Aragonite smiled back. "Heard a human say it once, always wanted to use it."

Julie laughed again, feeling her energy lighten a little. She finished getting dressed, then steeled herself to face whatever the day would bring. She was glad that Sarah had put a stop to Ben's idea of going back in time to change things. Even though she highly doubted it was even possible, she really didn't want to lose her life here with her beautiful children and her Flame. If she had lived forever in Atlantis, she would have been alone for eternity.

"I'm glad too," Aragonite said, echoing her thoughts. "After waiting so long to be with you, I have no intention of losing you."

Julie held out her arms and he reached out to embrace her. She breathed in his woodsy scent and closed her eyes. She could understand why the men had created the machine though. Because she would give anything to live in this moment for eternity.

But right now, she had a job to do.

"I'll see you in a bit, are you coming in for breakfast?"

"Maybe after I've got the kids to school. I better hustle them." Aragonite leaned down to kiss her, then left. Julie sighed. She left the cabin and headed for the house, walking slowly and trying to notice the beauty around her, as though it would create a protective armour for her, keeping the negative energies out.

She was joined by Saphron and Vivi just outside the house. They both looked as apprehensive as she felt.

"Hey, are you guys okay, did you sleep okay?" she asked, slipping into hostess mode.

They both nodded. "I think so, still not used to how quiet it is here," Vivi said.

Julie chuckled, and the three women headed inside. "I know what you mean, it took me weeks to get used to that."

Saphron and Vivi sat down at the tables in the front room, and began helping themselves to cereal. Julie went through to the kitchen, and found Violet there, in a flurry of activity, making pancakes.

"Hey," she said. "Can I help?"

Violet glanced up and Julie could see that she'd barely slept. "Yes, that would be great, if you could take note of what people want, I will do the cooking. And if you could sort out drinks and stuff too that would be good."

Julie nodded and got the kettle boiling, then went to ask Saphron and Vivi if they wanted anything cooked. She passed Greg on her way, and he looked just as awful as

Violet. She smiled at him and he nodded before making his way to the kitchen.

Julie busied herself with the breakfast rush, but her heart was aching for her two friends, and she really hoped that they would be able to find a way through this.

When everyone had arrived and was served, she sat down in the kitchen to eat her own breakfast. Violet joined her.

"You okay?" she asked quietly.

Violet sighed, and wiped her sweaty forehead with her sleeve. "I guess. I couldn't sleep last night. Everything just kept going around in my head. I just can't get past the fact that my guests this weekend are the reason why I lost everything in Atlantis. Why we all lost everything." She shook her head. "My heart hurts just thinking about it. And I have to admit, even though Sarah vetoed the idea, I want to go back. I want to have my life there back. I want to grow old and watch my daughter grow up."

Julie frowned. "You'd give all of this up? Really? It would be as though none of this had ever happened. The Academy, this life here, all the lives since Atlantis… you'd really give them all up to have that life back?"

Violet nodded. "I was so happy there. I had everything I needed, and was about to have the thing I wanted most in the world, a child. And it was all cruelly ripped away from me. I want it back. All of it." A tear slid down her cheek, and Julie began to worry that Violet might try to convince the others that they should go back.

Aragonite entered the kitchen, and her heart constricted. She wouldn't give up her life here, it was her turn to be with her Flame.

She looked at Violet. "I'm afraid that I don't wish to go back, and I would speak up and say so, if it were to become a possibility."

Violet blinked at her. "Oh, don't worry, Sarah was quite firm, and although I'm hurting, I understand. Even though I might not consciously remember, my soul would know that I took away the lives of millions of people, and I couldn't live with that."

She took her plate to the sink, and smiled at Julie. "Mind helping me clear up? Then we women can do a nice closing ceremony while the men do whatever they want to."

There was a note of bitterness in her tone, but Julie nodded. She swallowed the last bit of pancake. "I'll clear the tables."

Aragonite, who had been quietly observing their conversation followed her out the kitchen. "I'll give you a hand."

* * *

"Promise me that you guys won't decide to change the past, and go against Sarah's wishes?" Lisa said to Joseph after breakfast, before they went to attend the last meditations.

"I promise. As much as Atlantis was beautiful, I wouldn't choose to go back. I was miserable there with my wife, and I wouldn't want to live an eternity with her."

Lisa frowned. "But you took part in creating the machine?"

"I guess maybe I did so in the hope I might live long enough to meet someone else," Joseph shrugged. "Who knows? It was a very different world back then."

Lisa nodded and slipped on a warmer cardigan. "True.

I must admit, I enjoyed being a healer there, although, the machine would have put me out of business, by the sounds of it."

Joseph chuckled. "Yes it would, I still feel amazing now, actually. The effects of it even through the meditation were palpable."

"Could you not just bring back the design? So the machine could be created now?"

Joseph frowned. "You want me to make a machine that is designed to make us live eternally but is likely to malfunction and destroy the planet? Um, no, I don't think that's a good idea?"

"Oh, yeah, I keep forgetting about that bit."

Joseph shook his head. "I think the past is best where it is – in the past. I don't know what this weekend was meant to achieve, but so far it seems to have just stirred up trouble."

Lisa sighed. "Yes, it has, but hopefully it will end your nightmares? Now that you know the truth of what happened?"

"I hope so. For your sake as well as mine, I know you haven't got nearly enough sleep recently." He pulled her into his arms and kissed her slowly, making her heart flutter. She glanced at the neatly made bed and he laughed, reading her mind.

"We haven't got time, but later, I promise."

She groaned. "Fine. I'll hold you to that."

"You better!"

She smiled at her Flame, then left the pod, and made her way down the leaf strewn path to the meditation tent. She shivered in the damp autumn air. She hoped it would be nice and cosy inside.

Maggie, Saphron, Vivi, Julie and Sarah were all waiting for her. Along with Ruby, Beatrice and Amy. "Hey! When did you lovely ladies get here?"

"Just now," Amy said with a smile. "Violet sent us messages last night, and I couldn't resist spending time here with you all."

"And also getting a break from the kids!" Beatrice added with a grin.

Lisa frowned. "Ben is here as well though, who has them?"

"Oh, they're in school, I'll have to go after this."

Lisa smiled. "Well it's good to see you."

"Okay, so I was chatting to Sarah this morning," Violet said, addressing the whole circle of women. "And I thought it would be a good idea to move away from all the revelations that we discovered this weekend, and to instead focus on the present moment. Going back in time to change the past may seem like a brilliant idea, but in truth, how do we know if it will in fact bring us the lives we really want? So I want to hold a manifestation circle with you all this morning. Think of one thing that you wish to manifest, then we will each share our desires in turn, and then as a group we will focus on each one. This tray," she said, pointing to the empty tea tray in the middle of the circle. "Is our point of focus. Imagine the thing arriving on the tray. Of course, it is unlikely to, but as we know, when we use this very concentrated focus, things do tend to manifest very quickly. So be sure to ask for what you truly want, that will enhance your life." Violet finished speaking and smiled.

"Now who would like to go first?"

CHAPTER NINETEEN

The men had all agreed to adhere to Sarah's wishes. After all, how could they defy the Angel of Destiny? But they had also all wished to return to Atlantis to experience their fondest memories, to be there one last time, as it was unlikely the men would ever gather again in this lifetime. Also, Jack had been eager to see more of Atlantis in order to add to his sketches. He hoped to do a series of paintings of the Golden City.

Greg found himself wandering from memory to memory, absorbing every moment spent with Velvet, and with other souls he had known and loved in Atlantis. He stayed away from the painful memories, and spent some time with the machine before it malfunctioned. He found himself in the room with it, and he glanced at his desk and frowned. In the memory with Jack, he had been working on modifications, on improvements, but had stopped when Jack told him to. But there had been more drawings there than that. Where had the rest gone? He went to the desk and rifled through his sketches, and found that several were missing. Where had they gone? He resolved to ask the others if they had taken them for some reason. He had no idea why they would, but it was odd that they were missing.

He slipped into another memory, where he was sat in the main room of their home on the beach, listening to Violet playing the song she wrote for him.

She glanced over at him, and smiled, her eyes shining with pure love for him, and he sighed, wondering if he would ever see her look at him that way again.

The memory faded and he found himself in the water, looking back to the stormy shore where Velvet's lifeless body lay. He was about to turn and dive under, feeling short of breath, when he saw a figure approach Velvet's body. He frowned. He thought that most souls had chosen to become Merpeople. Who was it?

He squinted, but couldn't make out their features. The memory faded, and he slipped under the water.

He opened his eyes and gasped quietly. He looked around the room to find that everyone else was already back, their eyes open.

"Are you okay?" Jack asked.

He nodded. "I think so. Did anyone see anything new? And does anyone remember taking my drawings? Some of my designs went missing."

Everyone shook their heads. "Are you sure?" Dylan asked. "Maybe they just weren't in the memory?"

Greg sighed. "I don't know, something was just, off. There was someone on the beach too, when I left for the sea, and Violet was gone. But I couldn't see who it was." He rubbed his eyes. "It's probably nothing. Unless anyone has anything more to share, I just want to say a thank you to all of you for coming this weekend, it has certainly been interesting, and I hope that this knowledge will serve to help you heal, rather than burden you with guilt. We may have created the machine that destroyed Atlantis, but our intention was to create something beautiful, and I hope you can hold true to that intention, and forgive yourself for the part you may have played."

"Have you forgiven yourself?" Jack asked him softly.

Greg shook his head. "Not yet, but I hope to. One day." He smiled. "Maybe when Violet has forgiven me."

Jack nodded. "I will send everyone a note when I have completed the paintings, if you would like to see them?"

"Oh yes, that would be good, please do," Henry said.

"Yes, I'd like to see them too," Dylan agreed.

"Okay, let's go get some lunch, I have some curry ready-made."

"Oh that sounds amazing," Ben said, getting to his feet. "I kept seeing all the amazing food I used to eat in Atlantis and I'm starving now!"

Greg led the men downstairs, and busied himself in the kitchen, heating up the curry and cooking some rice. The lingering feeling that someone else had played a part in the destruction of Atlantis stayed at the edges of his consciousness, but by the time the food was ready and the women had returned to the house, it had faded away.

* * *

Astrid squeezed Xander's hand a little tighter, as they walked to their favourite restaurant. It was dark already, but the streets were well lit.

"I'm glad you suggested going out tonight, I have to admit, I'm running out of meal ideas," she said.

Xander smiled. "Yeah I thought you deserved a break, besides, we should go out more often, life's too short not to relax and have fun."

Astrid frowned. "I really wish you would stop saying that. Nothing has happened, despite your premonitions. The world is still the crazy place it has always been, there's been no big events or anything, perhaps the Angels were wrong? The cards were wrong?"

Xander sighed and they both stepped out into the street to dodge around a slow dog walker. "I really hope that is the case, though I'd feel bad for all the readings I gave last week where I basically told people to live as though they would be dead next week."

"Oh dear," Astrid said, trying to sound serious but finding it quite funny. "What if they all went out and bought expensive cars and clothes, thinking it wouldn't matter anyway?"

Xander grinned at her. "Is that what you would do? If you didn't have long to live? You'd go on a spending spree?"

Astrid laughed. "No, probably not. I would go and see all my family, and old friends from school and uni. And I would try and see some of the places on my bucket list. Do you know, I still haven't been to Glastonbury?"

"Seriously? You haven't lived, woman! Fine, let's go tomorrow."

"What? It's hours away! Are you mad?"

"No," Xander said as he opened the door to the restaurant and ushered her inside. "But I would hate for either of us to die with any regrets. We can see your family and mine along the way."

"Okay. Do we have to see yours though?" she teased.

Xander chuckled. "Hmm, good point. We'll just stay for ten minutes."

They were seated by the waiter, and both picked up their menus.

"Five," Astrid said.

"Deal."

* * *

"And so, that's what I would like to leave with you all tonight. That just because you have lost a limb, doesn't mean that you now have to go out and become a superhero. You don't have to raise money for charity, or become a marathon runner, or even a motivational speaker," Tadhg paused, and there were a few chuckles in the room. "You can just live a normal life. You can follow the dreams you had before you lost a limb. You may need some modifications. You may need extra help. But you can be yourself." He smiled. "Thank you."

There was a round of applause and Tadhg breathed deeply. It was only his second gig, speaking to a group for a charity called LimbPower. The audience was mostly made up of children and young adults, and so seemed far more nerve-wracking than his first gig, which was to a much smaller group of adults.

But they seem to have been receptive to his story. He just made sure to keep his language in check. He chatted to a few of the group afterwards, then smiled as Lily and Hattie joined him at the front of the room. Hattie was clutching her doll, who had graduated to having a mini prosthetic, which had taken Tadhg hours to make.

"You were amazing," Lily said, kissing him on the cheek. "Everyone I've spoken to really enjoyed it. They love that you are advocating following your dreams, and not allowing the loss of a limb to dictate your choices."

"Although I never had any dreams before it happened," Tadhg said with a grin. "In a weird way, losing a limb was my wake up call. Without it, I would still be a grumpy old bast-"

"Tadhg! That was fantastic! Thank you so much for agreeing to speak. We really enjoyed it, may I book you again?"

Lily took Hattie's shoulder and they wandered away, while Tadhg chatted with the organiser about doing another gig in the future.

Although it had seemed like a huge gamble, starting a new career, it would seem that it had definitely paid off. He couldn't wait until he was earning enough to give Lily the chance to do less shifts, and enjoy life a little bit more.

He finished talking with the organiser, and then searched the room for his family. He had promised to take them out for a nice meal after the gig, and now that his nerves had subsided, his stomach was growling.

"Ready to eat?"

Tadhg turned to find Lily at his side, with Hattie on her hip.

"Definitely. Let's go."

He took Lily's hand, and they went out to the car. Once seated and buckled in, Lily reached across to touch his knee.

"I'm really, really proud of you."

Tadhg looked at his Flame, and smiled. "Thank you."

*   *   *

"What a strange weekend," Gold commented, breaking the silence in the car as Sarah drove them home on Monday afternoon.

"It was indeed that," Sarah agreed. "I really had no idea why we needed to be there, but I can see now that it was to stop them from trying to change the past. I mean, can you even imagine what the world would be like if they had changed the fate of Atlantis?"

"It might have been a lot better, actually," Gold said.

Sarah glanced at him, eyebrows raised. "Really? We wouldn't be here right now. My children wouldn't exist. This world would be an entirely different place."

"Their souls would still exist. They would just be on their own planets, rather than stuck here. Think about it. If Atlantis had continued, their wisdom would have spread, and right now we would have a sustainable future. Whereas currently, we will be lucky to have a future at all."

Sarah was quiet for a while, considering his words. "Perhaps it was selfishness that made me stop them from trying, rather than considering the good of the planet." She sighed. "But I'm happy right now. And I don't want to give up what we have, or my family, so that the world can have a better chance."

"You're right," Gold said. "That is selfish of you. But then, why can you not be selfish? You are human now, after all."

"You're saying I was wrong. That I should have acted

from my capacity as an Angel, and not from my human limitations."

Gold was quiet for a moment before replying, which was all the reply Sarah needed. "Perhaps. But there is no judgement. As I said before, I too am enjoying this life now. I would be loath to let it go just yet. Though in a few years, it is likely to be the case anyway. Alternatively, you are right. It would likely be too big a change and we would not know the true ramifications of such a change."

Sarah stared into the darkness, lit only by her headlights and the other cars passing them and she sighed. "It's done now. The Atlanteans will be unlikely to ever meet again, and it is only their combined energy that would have been powerful enough to cause this kind of shift." Gold stayed silent. "Right? Or do you still think there will be a shift?"

Gold frowned. "There is still something in the offing. But I have no idea what it might be. I don't think it will be down to the Atlanteans though, you are right about that."

Sarah slumped a little in her seat. Who else would be crazy enough to try and change the past? Her head hurt just thinking about all of the ripples and consequences.

"Shall we listen to some music?" Gold asked, reaching out to turn on the radio. The car was filled with the throbbing beat of dance music, and it was a welcome relief to allow her thoughts to dissipate.

She would worry about it all later.

CHAPTER TWENTY

"I love it here! Are you sure we have to go home?"

Sam rolled his eyes at Saphron. "You want to stay here in Glastonbury?"

"Yes! Don't you feel at home here? I do."

"That's because the place is full of witches," Henry commented as they passed a very colourfully dressed couple.

"Shh!" Vivi said, laughing. "Don't offend anyone, they might curse us!"

All four of them laughed, and headed to a café to get some lunch. It was pretty busy, but they managed to squeeze onto the end of a table for six, where a couple were already eating.

"I spoke to Louise. Her mum's funeral will be in two weeks' time. Bless her, she was in bits," Saphron heard the woman say to her partner.

"Do you want to see her? We really could skip seeing my folks, I don't mind."

"Could we? I do feel bad that I haven't seen her since she and Oscar reunited. Thank you, Xander, I'd love that."

Saphron snapped her attention back to her own company, as Sam was nudging her and asking her what she would like to order. She scanned the menu and chose the most British thing she could find, then went back to eavesdropping on the couple. For some reason, they seemed familiar, and she wondered if she might have met them before.

"At least I can tick this off my bucket list now," the woman said. "If the world does in fact end in the next few days, at least I can die happy knowing I've seen the Tor."

Saphron looked at Vivi, who was also eavesdropping and raised her eyebrows. Vivi looked equally as shocked.

"But I thought it was all going to be okay now?" Vivi half-whispered. Their Flames were chatting about work, oblivious to their hushed tones.

"So did I, but perhaps it isn't all over yet?"

Vivi frowned, and Saphron hated to see her usually bubbly friend look so sad.

"There's nothing more we can do about it now. Let's just enjoy the rest of our trip. We'll be at Stonehenge tomorrow, aren't you excited?"

A smile returned to Vivi's face, and she glanced at the couple again, but Saphron could see the tension easing from her features.

"Yes, I am. It's a shame we won't be able to touch the stones, but I am excited."

A few minutes later, their food arrived, and they all tucked in, and discussed their plans for the rest of their vacation. As she ate, Saphron put out a silent prayer to the Angels that they would return home safely, and that the woman's comment had meant nothing.

* * *

"I really don't need to see a doctor," Maggie insisted. "Please stop fussing. It was a vision that gave me the funny turn, and I'm just getting a bit of a cold, I think. Just got a bit chilled through, that's all."

Steve held his hands up in defeat. "Okay, okay. It was just a very full on weekend, and you really worried me."

Maggie sighed. "I know, but I'm fine, I promise. I'm just going to go meditate for a bit, I need to process some of the weekend's revelations. And I need to do some clearing. I really did struggle being around that many people."

Steve hugged her and kissed her briefly on the lips. "Okay. I'll start dinner. Helen and Chad will be over soon with the kids. Unless you want me to cancel?"

Maggie shook her head. "No, it's fine. It will be good to see them, actually. Just give me half an hour, okay?"

Steve nodded and released her, and she went to her office and closed the door behind her. In truth, she was utterly exhausted, and in no fit state to entertain, but she hoped that with a bit of quiet time, she might regain some of her energy.

She sat on her meditation cushion and crossed her legs, then lit the candle in front of her, as a point of focus. Her gaze blurred and her mind drifted, and she remembered the final circle the women had held at the retreat, and all the desires they had wished to manifest. When it had come to be her turn, all she could think of was that she truly wanted to fulfil her mission, her purpose on this planet. But when asked what that was, she had to admit, that she wasn't really sure.

She let her mind wander, and she got a glimpse of the

vision again, of Violet being sad and alone, and she got flickers of similar things happening to the other Flames. She saw relationships deteriorate, and the world descending into darkness. She sighed. Had they really failed? Was the world ever going to see the dawn of the first Golden Age? Were they all just going to return home?

Suddenly, a new vision appeared. It was so vibrant and detailed, and so unlike anything Maggie had ever seen before, that she was a little taken aback. But clear as day, she could see it, she could see the Golden Age.

Maggie brought herself back to the present moment, and smiled. She now knew what her purpose was, and she knew exactly how to fulfil it.

* * *

"Did you think Maggie seemed a little strange tonight?" Helen asked Chad as they drove home later that night.

Chad frowned, but kept his eyes on the road. "Strange? In what way? She was really tired, considering all the stuff that happened at the Retreat this weekend, it's not surprising is it?"

"I guess, but it wasn't just fatigue, she kept telling the kids she loved them, and I swear she hugged me way more times than she usually does." Helen glanced back to check on the kids, but they were fast asleep. It was past their bedtime, but Helen had found it difficult to leave.

"I guess she did seem a little more affectionate than usual. Did you ask her if she was okay?"

Helen shook her head. "Didn't really get a chance. What did Steve think of your weather theories?" she asked, changing the subject.

"He thought they were interesting. He'd also noticed that the weather seemed to be quite extreme. But maybe it was being stirred up by the shifts at the moment."

"Maybe. At least we're not going to wake up tomorrow in different realms. I can't believe they actually considered going back to Atlantis and changing it!"

"I know. I wouldn't even be on this planet if they had."

Helen shuddered. "I'm so pleased Sarah put a stop to it." She reached over to squeeze his knee. "I'm so glad to be here with you."

Chad smiled. "Me too. But I am a little worried about the future. It all seems so volatile right now. That in any moment, there could be this cataclysmic event that changes our lives forever."

"I know what you mean. But maybe that just means we should enjoy every moment as much as we can. We can't live in fear of the future. Otherwise we might actually create the things we fear the most."

"You're right. Let's just enjoy the moment, and plan the future that we want to experience."

Helen smiled. "Yes, let's do that."

* * *

Charlie woke up with a gasp, and sat bolt upright in bed.

"What? What is it?" Ceri asked, waking suddenly with the movement and noise. She looked at him with concern as he continued to gasp for breath.

"A dream, just a dream," he gasped out.

Ceri shook her head. "It's more than that. You look like you've seen a ghost. And this is the fourth time this week you've woken up in a sweat. What's going on?"

Charlie met her gaze, and then bowed his head. "I'm afraid to tell you."

She reached out to lift his chin, so that she could look him in the eye. "Tell me. Please. Because you're scaring me, and I don't think anything you could say would be worse than my imagination."

Charlie sighed and closed his eyes.

"I keep dreaming of Atlantis."

"Atlantis?"

Charlie opened his eyes to see the puzzled look on Ceri's face. "Yes, I had a life there." He sighed. "I will lend you a book that will explain in more detail but essentially, I was in Atlantis, and so was Violet. Only her name was Velvet then."

He could see confusion and suspicion on Ceri's face, probably because he had never mentioned his interest in Atlantis or Earth Angels before, but he ploughed on anyway. "I was in love with her. Desperately. Madly, really. And yet, I couldn't be with her. She was with her Twin Flame, Laguz."

"Twin Flame?" Ceri mouthed, obviously having questions, but not wanting to interrupt him completely.

"Yes. Like a soulmate. And they were very much in love. And I couldn't bear it. I was sick with jealousy. I wanted her for myself." He sighed. "But it was never going to happen."

"So what happens in the nightmares?" Ceri asked, still looking confused.

"I found out that Laguz and a group of men were creating something. A machine that would give us all everlasting life. That would make us immortals. Some of the men were doing it because they wanted to be gods, but Laguz, he was doing it because he wanted to be with Velvet, forever." Charlie hung his head. "I just couldn't bear the thought of living forever, but never getting to be with her. And I was too selfish to just take myself out of the equation, so I sabotaged it."

Ceri's eyebrows shot up. "The machine?"

"Yes. I stole some drawings, worked out where the weaknesses were, and I caused it to malfunction. In truth, I hadn't really thought through the implications, I just wanted it to stop working. But instead, it caused the destruction of Atlantis."

Ceri frowned, and Charlie could see she was having trouble digesting his words. "You destroyed Atlantis?"

Charlie nodded. "Yes. It was a real place, that existed before I destroyed it. And in doing so, I killed her. I killed Velvet. And her unborn child. Laguz left for the oceans as a Merperson, and I was still cradling Velvet's dead body when the machine exploded."

Tears were running down Ceri's cheeks, and Charlie wasn't sure if she was crying because of fear and confusion, his loss, or because she was regretting falling in love with such a monstrous human being.

"I shouldn't have told you," he whispered. "What must you think of me? I'm not only a murderer in this life, but I destroyed an entire civilisation. How can you possibly love me?"

Ceri reached out and pulled him into her arms, and suddenly Charlie began to sob. The pain of losing Violet, of the guilt of his actions, and then of being loved by such a pure soul, when he honestly didn't think he deserved it, came pouring out, and he cried harder than he had ever cried in his whole life.

"You're different now," Ceri whispered into his ear. "You would never be able to feel this pain if you didn't regret your actions. You were in love, and people do stupid things when they're in love."

"Like forgive a murderer and marry him anyway?" Charlie choked out.

Ceri chuckled through her own tears. "Yes. Exactly."

"So you believe me? That it was real, it wasn't just a dream?"

"I believe your feelings are real," Ceri said carefully. "I don't know anything about Atlantis, but I do know you, and I believe you are hurting right now, and that you are sorry for what happened."

After a few moments, Charlie's sobs calmed, and the tears slowed. He took the tissues that Ceri offered him and blew his nose. "What do I do now? How can I live with this?"

"You just do. It happened a very long time ago, and there's nothing we can do about it now. I would ask the Angels for forgiveness, and then let it go."

Charlie nodded, but his heart still felt heavy. The memory of Velvet's lifeless body flashed through his mind and he choked back another sob.

"I still love you, Charlie. And nothing, I mean nothing, will ever stop me from loving you."

"I love you too. Thank you for not thinking I'm a monster."

Ceri laughed again. "You're not a monster. You just a man. A man who has made mistakes."

CHAPTER TWENTY-ONE

Linen hugged the woman tightly, and tried his best not to cry. In the short few weeks they had been on the island, the people they were helping had become like a family to them, and he knew he would miss them when they left.

Aria was waiting for him, clutching the makeshift cat carrier in her hand. He knew she hated goodbyes even more than he did.

"We will keep in touch," he assured the woman, smiling at her as he let go. He joined Aria and picked up the duffel bag that contained both their possessions, and they began walking to the airport, which had returned to full functionality, allowing them to get a normal flight out of there.

"You okay?" he asked Aria.

"Yeah," she said, but her small face was sad. "I just feel so bad. I mean, we can just walk away, we can just go home. But these people can't. This is their home. They have nowhere else to go."

Linen sighed. "I know. But it is time we went home,

don't you think? And we've managed to sort out taking Storm with us too, so that's a good thing isn't it? We will make sure he is taken care of now."

Aria smiled and peered into the carrier. "Yes, thank you for sorting that out. I would have been even more upset if I'd had to leave him behind."

"So what's the first thing we'll do, do you think, when we get back to the UK?"

Aria thought for a few moments, then smiled. "I want to eat a whole big bar of chocolate, and then sleep."

Linen chuckled. That was the Aria he knew and loved. "Sounds good to me, sign me up."

Aria giggled. "Chocolate does make everything better, although the stuff we found in America was disgusting."

Linen smiled. "Yeah, it was."

They reached the small airport and entered. It was stiflingly hot in there, on account of the air conditioning not being fixed yet.

"Have you had any more nightmares?" Aria asked, as Linen rifled through the rucksack for their passports and tickets.

"No," he replied. "I haven't."

"Oh good," Aria said. "I guess the world isn't ending just yet after all then."

* * *

Lisa awoke with a start, as something or someone was licking her all over her face rather enthusiastically. "What the hell?" she exclaimed, opening her eyes and sitting upright. The tiny black puppy gazed back at her, and her eyes widened.

"Where did you come from?" she asked, reaching out to pick it up. She clutched the small pup to her chest, and noticed it had a pink ribbon around its neck, and attached to the ribbon was an engagement ring. She squealed, and untied the ribbon, taking the diamond encrusted platinum band from it, and slipping it onto her ring finger.

"Is that a yes then?" Joseph asked from the doorway.

She looked up and nodded. Still clutching the puppy to her chest, she jumped out of bed and went to him, and wrapped her free arm around her Flame, kissing him hard.

"How did you know though?" she asked, when their lips parted. "Did one of the girls tell you?"

Joseph frowned. "Tell me what?"

Lisa lifted up the puppy, who started to lick her face again. "This is what I said I wanted. In our manifestation circle. I wanted another dog, and I wanted to marry you."

Joseph laughed in surprise. "Seriously? You asked for those things specifically?"

"Yes. We were only meant to ask for one thing, but I couldn't decide what I wanted more, you, or a dog." She grinned up at him and he smiled.

"She is rather cute, I have to admit. What are you going to name her?"

"It's a girl?" Lisa asked. "Oh, well, pink ribbon, of course." She lifted up the puppy to look her in the eyes. "What should I name you, little one?"

"While you decide, would you like some breakfast?"

Lisa nodded. "Yes please." She grabbed her dressing gown and followed him to the kitchen still carrying the puppy.

She sat on the bar stool and the puppy snuggled into

her fleece robe.

"I wonder if anyone else's desires manifested this quickly?" she wondered out loud.

"What did the others ask for?" Joseph asked, getting out the frying pan.

Lisa shook her head. "Sorry, we all swore we wouldn't tell anyone outside the circle. Which is why I was so surprised by this little one this morning."

"Fair enough. I won't ask any more questions. I guess you'll just have to wait and see if theirs come true or not?"

"Yeah," Lisa said, stroking the puppy's soft head. "I guess I will."

* * *

Violet watched Greg sleeping, and she wondered if she was making a huge mistake allowing him to be close to her again, and forgiving him for what happened, all those lifetimes ago. She wondered if she should have left him, but then it seemed like more of a punishment for her to lose him all over again.

She sighed. Despite the feelings of anger and hatred that had arisen, she still couldn't imagine her life without him by her side, which was why she had lied to him. All that time ago in Atlantis, when he had offered to change everyone into Merpeople, so that she could live, she had insisted that it had to be her, but she was lying. He could have done it. But she knew he would die in the process, and she couldn't live without him. So in fact, it was her who chose to let their child die, and to die herself, just so that she wouldn't have to live without him. Maybe that was why she had felt so angry with him. Because really, she was angry with herself.

She stroked his face gently, and he stirred a little in his sleep. She thought about the request she had made to her circle of friends. The one thing that she wished to manifest, to make her life the best it could possibly be. Though it had to be far too early to tell, she had felt familiar stirrings within her, and she was almost certain that it was indeed going to manifest, if it hadn't already begun to. It was this new development that had released her anger, and softened her heart to him again.

Violet wondered whether she should tell him, but she wanted to wait until she was certain first, so not to raise his hopes. She leaned over to kiss him gently, then she slipped out from under the covers and put her dressing gown on. It was their first day off since the retreat, and she wanted to make him breakfast in bed, just to show that she was no longer holding a grudge. And also because they very rarely got to spend time together, just the two of them, and she was looking forward to having a whole day.

She pottered about in the kitchen, making cups of tea, and was just about to butter the toast when a voice behind her made her jump.

"Violet, it's for you."

She spun around to see Greg standing there, holding out her phone. "Oh! You scared me!" She put the toast down and wiped her hands, then took the phone from him. She glanced at the screen. It was Maggie's number.

"Maggie?" she said, putting the phone to her ear. "Are you okay?" She glanced at the clock, it wasn't even eight yet.

"Hi, Violet, it's Steve."

Violet frowned, his voice sounded weird. "Steve, what's

wrong? Is Maggie okay?"

"No, she's not. She's, she's..." he broke off, and Violet's heart stopped for a moment at the sound of his sobs.

"Steve?" she whispered. "Steve, tell me, please."

"She's dead, Violet. She's gone."

Tears filled Violet's eyes and her knees went weak. She began to sink to the floor and felt Greg's arms encircle her, holding her up. "No, she can't be. What happened? When?"

"Last night. She killed herself."

Everything went grey, and the last thing Violet remembered before blacking out was the sound of her phone hitting the floor.

EPILOGUE

"Thank you all for coming today. Before we start the movie, which I know is what you've all come here to see, I would like to just talk a little about an amazing woman, who was my dearest friend, who I know was so looking forward to this day."

Violet smiled at the audience in the small theatre, and did her best to hold back her tears. It was a private showing of her movie, *The Earth Angel Training Academy,* and she had invited fifty of her closest friends and family to watch it with her, as she had only been able to take Greg to the bigger premieres.

"Maggie was a beautiful soul. We have lived through many lifetimes as friends, and in fact, she is one of the characters in my book, and in the movie we are about to watch. She was a Seer, and she would often have visions of the future, and sometime of the past. She has helped, supported and guided me in this life, and I am so very grateful to her. She told me once, months ago, that she had a vision of the future, and that we were all there, together, in the end," she paused to breathe, struggling to keep her composure.

"But it seems it was not meant to be." Violet smoothed her dress over her bump, and her heart broke at the thought that her child would never meet Maggie. And that her friend would never know, that aside from losing her, Violet was the happiest she had been since Atlantis, having finally got everything she ever wanted.

"So, I would like to dedicate this movie to Maggie. A wonderful friend, an amazing Seer, and the most beautiful soul." She raised her champagne glass, which actually contained sparkling apple juice. "To Maggie."

Everyone in the audience held up their glasses. "To Maggie." They chorused.

Violet smiled, and a few tears managed to escape. "Thank you. Now, enjoy the show."

She left the platform at the front, and returned to her seat next to Greg. He reached out to take her hand, and gripped it tightly in his.

"That was beautiful. I'm sure she is watching right now, and she's really proud of you," Greg whispered.

Violet nodded but couldn't speak. She turned her attention to the screen, where the opening credits were rolling.

She only hoped that her Flame was right.

About the Author

Michelle lives in the UK, when she's not flitting in and out of other realms. She is an avid crafter, and enjoys letterpress printing, knitting, sewing, crochet, photography and many other creative pursuits. She has so far written fifteen novels for adults, one for children, a poetry collection and a self-help book.

Please feel free to write a review of this book. Michelle loves to get direct feedback, so if you would like to contact her, please e-mail **theamethystangel@hotmail.co.uk** or keep up to date by following her blog – **TwinFlameBlog.com.** You can also follow her on Twitter **@themiraclemuse** or on Instagram **@michellegordonauthor**

To sign up to her mailing list, visit:
michellegordon.co.uk

GRATITUDE

The one thing I am most grateful for, is that I get to keep doing this. That I get to keep writing, and publishing my writing, and I am so very blessed to be surrounded by people who think that it's a good idea!

These people are the reason I was even able to begin this journey in the first place, and they are definitely why I am able to continue on this journey, because they are able to convince me it's a good idea too.

There have been some new additions to my life this year, and there are some who have left my life this year. 2017 has been an interesting one to say the least!

Lily and Toby, thank you for the opportunity to house sit your place in Cornwall, where I began writing this book, and where I had some much needed time out!

Thank you, Cerian and Annie from The Cwtch in Abergavenny. Your support and enthusiasm for the Unicorn book has been amazing, and it's because of your encouragement that this book has come to fruition so quickly! I really appreciate your friendship and am looking forward to see what the next year brings us all.

Thank you, Crystal Dawne, for the opportunity to be a part of your amazing documentary on Angels - *The Illumined Ones*. It is such a beautiful, inspiring and uplifting film, and I think it will help a lot of people.

Thank you, lovely Patreon patrons, for your continued support. You are making this book possible! Thank you,

Kariel Tejai, Rachel Miller, Amanda Bigrell, Xander Holland, Ana Leon and Tiffany Hathorn.

So much love and gratitude to my dearest friends and supporters, the following people know just how much I love them, and how blessed I feel to have them in my life:

Sarah Rebecca Vine, Tiffany Hathorn, Robert Tremblay, Laurie Huston, George Hardwick, Fyn Day, Xander Holland, Lucja Fratczak-Kay, Andrew Embling, Kelly Draper, Helen Gordon, Niki Gilbert, Shelley-Nicole Brookdale, Rachel Miller, Mr Bee, Anabela Da Costa, Alex Lane, Becci Ann, Damien Cordell, Rachael Barnwell, Meera Virk, Lesley George, Kenny John, Miranda Adams, Margaux Joy DeNador, Neil Chard, Louise Sofia Weir, David Wetton, Philip James, Sharon Andrews, Jenni Riley, Trish Mclean, Adrian Incledon-Webber, Victor Keegan, Vikki Elizabeth Finlay and Claire Weeks.

Thank you to LimbPower and Cherished Gowns UK for inspiring parts of the story, please do visit their websites to see the amazing work they do: limbpower.com and cherishedgowns.org.uk

And finally, thank you to the three people who have believed in me the most, and believed in me the longest, and who have been there every step of the way on this journey of self-discovery and book writing and publishing:

My mum, Sally Byrne, my sister, Liz Gordon, and my best friend, Elizabeth Lockwood. I love you three so much, and I am beyond grateful that you are all in my life.

BOOKS BY MICHELLE GORDON

WHERE'S MY F**KING UNICORN?

Are your bookshelves filled with self-help books, and yet your life feels empty? Do you keep following paths to enlightenment that lead to the same dead ends? You've read the books, attended the seminars and taken heed of every bit of advice going... but you're still waiting for your f**king unicorn to come along! Where's My F**king Unicorn? is a guide to life, creativity and happiness that offers a very different way forward.

Author, Michelle Gordon, explains why, in spite of all your best efforts, your life still doesn't live up to your vision of what it should be, and tells you exactly what you can do about it. In refreshingly down-to-earth language, she shows you how to harness all the self-knowledge you have gained from all those self-help books you've read, and actually start putting it to practical use.

Where's My F**king Unicorn? is published by *Ammonite Press* and is available online and in bookstores.

THE GIRL WHO LOVED TOO MUCH

What would you do if you suddenly found yourself in a different reality that was better for you, but not for those you loved?

Caru loves to make things. And collect things. And give gifts. She loves to print, sew, knit, paint. Her life is full of unfinished projects, yet devoid of financial stability and romance. Though she loves her life, she finds herself disappointing people and struggling to keep everyone happy.

So when Caru wishes life could be simpler, and then finds herself in a completely different world, where her life is easy, money is abundant, and her long-term boyfriend is the most fabulous cook, she can't quite believe her luck.

But will all her wishes come true? Or will the dream turn into a nightmare?

The Girl Who Loved Too Much is a modern day 'It's a Wonderful Life'.

The Girl Who Loved Too Much is published by *Jasper Tree Press* and is available online in eBook and print.

THE OLD SOUL'S HANDBOOK

It's not easy being an Earth Angel on this planet.
I hope the words within these pages help you in whatever situation you find yourself in.
Simply ask a question or for guidance, and then open the book to a random page.
The answers are within.

The Earth Angel Series is published by
The Amethyst Angel and is available online in eBook and print.

Not From This Planet is an Independent Publisher on a mission to collaborate with authors to create the best possible books that delight and inspire and entertain – and also pay a fair royalty to the author. They treat every book as if it were their own and they have big have plans to take the publishing world by storm.

Follow Not From This Planet on
Instagram - @notfromthisplanetbooks
Facebook - @notfromthisplanetbooks
Twitter - @ NFTPbooks

NotFromThisPlanet.co.uk

www.ingramcontent.com/pod-product-compliance
Lightning Source LLC
Chambersburg PA
CBHW071342080526
44587CB00017B/2927